VGM Opportunities Series

OPPORTUNITIES IN
JOURNALISM
CAREERS

Donald L. Ferguson
Jim Patten

Revised edition

Foreword by
Morley Safer
CBS News

VGM Career Books

Library of Congress Cataloging-in-Publication Data

Ferguson, Donald L.
    Opportunities in journalism careers / Donald L. Ferguson and Jim Patten ;
foreword by Morley Safer. — Rev. ed.
        p. cm. — (VGM opportunities series)
    ISBN 0-658-01050-6 (hardcover)
    ISBN 0-658-01051-4 (paperback)
        1. Journalism—Vocational guidance—United States. I. Patten,
Jim. II. Title. III. Series.

PN4797 .F48 2001
070.4'023'73—dc21

00-53372

Cover photograph copyright © PhotoDisc

Published by VGM Career Books
A division of The McGraw-Hill Companies.
4255 West Touhy Avenue, Lincolnwood (Chicago), Illinois 60712-1975 U.S.A.
Copyright © 2001 by The McGraw-Hill Companies.
Printed in the United States of America
International Standard Book Number: 0-658-01050-6 (hardcover)
                                     0-658-01051-4 (paperback)

1   2   3   4   5   6   7   8   9   0   LB/LB   0   9   8   7   6   5   4   3   2   1

CONTENTS

Getting hooked on journalism. Compensation expectations. Job satisfaction. It's not about being popular.

A job that endures. Newspapers in Colonial America. Freedom of the press. The development of modern newspapers. The electronic media. Ethical standards for journalists. Journalists' functions. The history of Canadian journalism.

Spelling—a sixth sense? A learnable skill.

Reporters. Copy editors. Layout and page designers. Editors. Columnists. Editorial cartoonists. Editorial writers. Photographers.

ABOUT THE AUTHORS

Donald L. Ferguson and Jim Patten both have extensive experience in the wide-ranging field of journalism.

Ferguson has held various media and related journalism positions. He has worked for newspapers and has taught high school journalism and college journalism at Ohio State University, the University of Nebraska, and Baylor University. He provided public relations services for the Lincoln, Nebraska, school system and formed his own consulting firm, working with school districts and education associations throughout the United States. He managed a Denver-based public relations, advertising, and opinion research firm. Ferguson has provided public relations services for Fortune 500 corporations and has been recognized for his expertise in crisis communications and investor relations by *Inside PR* magazine.

Patten is head of the journalism department at the University of Arizona in Tucson. During his journalistic career, he worked as reporter, editor, photographer, editorial writer, and columnist at nine newspapers.

He previously taught at the University of Nebraska, Midland (Texas) College, and the University of Texas at El Paso. Patten also serves as writing coach for professional journalists and is active in high school press issues. He is an award-winning teacher active in many professional journalistic groups.

Ferguson and Patten are co-authors of *Journalism Today!, The Journalism Today! Workbook,* and *The Journalism Today! Teacher Resource Book,* published by NTC/Contemporary Publishing Group, Inc.

FOREWORD

I do not know of a single soul who fell into this line of work. It is not the kind of job that you might want to do, it is work that you must do. There are, for some, enormous financial rewards, but generally the reward is in the work itself.

I wanted to be a reporter from the age of sixteen and in the years since then, I cannot recall a moment of genuinely wishing to be anything else. There are no special gifts required to succeed. An ability to write clear, concise sentences is important, as is a slavish devotion to precision. By that I mean facts—not someone's interpretation of facts, but the genuine article. If you are too lazy or too sure of yourself to "go look it up," don't even think of becoming a reporter.

The most important gift is curiosity. You must have an insatiable hunger to know everything that is going on, from outer space to the locker room to behind the closed doors of the White House.

A reporter must have the ability to walk into perfect strangers' lives, ask the most personal kinds of questions, then leave without taking on their burdens. It does not mean that you become so hardened to human misery that you stop feeling. It simply means that you save those feelings for after hours, for your own time, if you have any.

The work can be difficult and debilitating, and the company you may have to keep may not be the most companionable. But when you get your teeth into a good story, and all the pieces fall into place, and the facts are there—cold, hard, and shining—there is nothing, no job quite like this one. Good hunting to those of you who choose journalism as a career.

Morley Safer
   CBS News

ACKNOWLEDGMENTS

For their assistance in the preparation of this book, the authors wish to thank:

G. Donald Gale
Jimmy D. Langham
Thomas Pendleton
Stephen A. Smith
Journalism Education Association, Inc.
Prof. Minko Sotiron
Accrediting Council on Education in Journalism and Mass Communication
Society of Professional Journalists
Our students, past, present, and future

CHAPTER 1

JOURNALISM: A WAY OF LIFE

Columnist James Kilpatrick told this story many years ago in *Quill* magazine, the official publication of the Society of Professional Journalists. A young man approached him for advice about becoming a newspaper reporter. Kilpatrick's visitor was eighteen, ready for college, and wanted to select a career. Should it be journalism?

Kilpatrick's response was: "Don't be a newspaperman if you possibly can help it." The young man was startled. Today, of course, the young man interested in journalism is just as likely (possibly even more likely) to be a young woman, and the career question more likely to be about television or an on-line medium. Kilpatrick's response, however, remains appropriate today.

Here's what he meant. Journalism is unlike any other craft. It most closely resembles show business. There's an undeniable element of ego in journalism, and an equally undeniable element of self-sacrifice. Performers know the show must go on. Journalists know the paper has to come out on time. They know the radio or TV newscast has to be ready when the camera's red light goes on. They also know that thousands of websites, many of them operated by media, are being updated all the time. If that means no day off this week, no coffee break tonight, no going home just because it's normal quitting time, those are the breaks. The work or "the public's interest" comes first.

GETTING HOOKED ON JOURNALISM

Journalists talk about attraction to their work as a calling, much the way ministers and surgeons do. Journalism is more than a job. It's a way of life. While sometimes it's exciting and exhilarating, it also can be grindingly difficult and at times boring. Don't be a journalist unless you can't help it.

Most journalists can't help it. They talk of "getting hooked" in a high school journalism class or after taking a news job not knowing what they were getting into. They talk about the adrenalin rush that comes with covering a big story. They dismiss worries about deadline pressure. "That's when it's really fun," they say. "When there's a big story and you're matching wits against the deadline, that's great. It's not pressure. It's hard to believe somebody is actually paying us to do this."

Some recent studies, however, show that newspeople do pay a price. They seem to suffer more stress on the job than do those in many other occupations. Many burn out before middle age and seek other careers. This worries some managers and the academics who do the studies. Yet journalism remains one of the most popular majors on most university campuses. Students see, and correctly so, the opportunity journalism provides for public service. Journalists affect the world.

So this book should carry a warning. Journalism can be addictive. Read on and face the possibility of getting hooked. If you don't *really* want the hard work of journalism, just say no now.

Some would-be journalists believe journalism is a glamorous life. There's a touch of truth to this. Some journalists uncover scandals that topple presidents and governors. Some cover Hollywood, Washington, DC, Ottawa, or other foreign capitals, and rub elbows with celebrities and heads of state. Some write columns or become television anchorpeople and get rich and famous. But for every journalist in that category, at least fifty work in quiet anonymity.

Look at your daily paper. Sure, it would be fun to be the reporter who wrote the lead story of the day, the one at the top of the front page. But there's much more to the newspaper than that. Look lower on the front page. See the little weather box with tomorrow's forecast? A journalist wrote that, too. See the index items, directing readers to stories inside? A journalist wrote them. Turn to the sports page. See the long lists in small type of all the scores from yesterday's games? A journalist compiled them. Some papers run school lunch menus. A journalist does that. Check the Sunday paper. See all those "home of the week" stories in the real estate section? A journalist wrote those stories. Glamorous? Hardly. But important and interesting to the people who read these newspapers? Definitely.

One of the real keys to journalistic success and contentment is to love the *process* of journalism regardless of its content or the medium by which it is conveyed. That means enjoying news work whether you're writing a routine street-closing notice or the weather forecast or a two-paragraph account of a basketball game in an outlying town. The process matters, and those "little" stories require the same degree of accuracy, the same attention to detail that the big stories do. Journalism isn't for you if you have to be a superstar.

A small story will illustrate the point. In the newsroom one day, the city editor opened an envelope from a public relations firm. In the envelope was a press release, a proposed story offered to the newspaper by the public relations people of a local company. The press release was too long and had extraneous information. The city editor looked around. He spotted the newest, youngest member of the staff. He gave her the press release and asked her to rewrite it into news form. She blew up. "Why should I have to do something like that?" she asked. She saw the light when a senior journalist in the room, a man with thirty years in the business, took her aside and explained to her that even with all his experience he would be *happy* to rewrite the press release if asked. No one in the newsroom, he told her, can be above doing any job if that's what the paper needs at that moment.

COMPENSATION EXPECTATIONS

When one of the authors of this book, then eighteen and much like the young man who approached Kilpatrick, told his high school journalism adviser that he had decided on a career in journalism, the adviser was pleased. "You won't make a lot of money but you'll sure have a lot of fun," he said. Today, both parts of that statement are less true than they used to be.

At one time journalists almost had to take an oath of poverty. It was the price they paid for being journalists, for being in on the action and seeing the world close-up. Some beginning journalists have been known to make so little money that they qualified for food stamps! One college textbook, published in the 1970s, actually stated that journalists can't make enough money to send their children to college.

This picture has changed. Although it is true that salaries of journalists are still too low, they're rising fast. At the top levels of management, fears have been expressed that unless salaries go up, journalism will lose the best and the brightest of the next generation, and the nation will suffer as a result. A new emphasis on improving the financial lot of journalists is at work—and working. While monetary compensation has always been an issue, today there are more job possibilities in journalism than ever before. Cable television, the Internet, and a boom in the corporate world, particularly in the high-tech arena, have created many new opportunities for journalists with solid credentials. Whether in broadcast or print journalism, public relations or marketing communications, demand for competent professionals is on the rise.

News-based television programs are everywhere on network and cable television. Of the growing number of cable channels, several have added news programming to their lineups. Like magazines, these media outlets are more specialized and can benefit from journalists who have a passion for the subject matter.

Salary Statistics

The starting salary for someone going into public relations just out of college is about $28,000 a year. A person starting in advertising sales can expect to make about $12,000 plus commissions. The new daily newspaper reporter will get about $25,000, and the new radio or television reporter between $20,000 and 25,000.

But these figures fall far short of telling the whole story. The beginning daily newspaper reporter lucky enough to land a job on an enlightened medium-sized daily (fifty thousand circulation or more) is likely to find his or her salary nearer to $30,000. Higher salaries are also possible in public relations, advertising, and radio and television. There are plenty of exceptions to the figures in the previous paragraph. And, of course, the figures represent *beginning* salaries only. Most journalists with a few years on the job do much better. Five years down the road, the journalist who started at $25,000 is apt to be making closer to $35,000. People in executive and management positions often make double or triple that.

But money is only one measure of job satisfaction. A study by the Dow Jones Newspaper Fund found that most recent graduates in mass media jobs were either moderately or very satisfied with their jobs.

What would cause this satisfaction?

JOB SATISFACTION

We said earlier that the high school adviser's statement about having fun probably isn't as true as it once was. That's correct. Journalists (and here we're including advertising and public-relations people) are more responsible than ever and are more concerned about ethics and truth—issues they struggle with daily. In the 1920s and during the days of so-called Jazz Journalism, journalists considered their role almost exclusively a way to entertain themselves and their readers, in that order. If that meant fudging a bit with the facts or exaggerating a story, no problem. Today no such spirit prevails. Today the rules require accuracy and responsibility. And that means harder work for people in mass media jobs.

Still, the workers like their work. Why? Because journalism remains a craft where honesty and integrity are admired—and required. Sure journalists compromise sometimes. No one and no job is perfect. But the central ethic remains: Serve the public with objective facts, honest advertising, and open and candid public relations. The nonobjective newspaper, magazine, or Internet story or newscast is soon rejected by the public. Not only is false advertising against the law, the fact is that it doesn't work. And the public-relations person who hides company wrongdoing and publicizes only the "good things" soon finds that he or she has lost credibility.

In the ideal world of the classroom, all journalists are honest. No advertisers can call the publisher or station manager and kill a story by threatening to take away their advertising. No journalist ever takes sides in a story. No story ever gets killed because it offends the local chamber of commerce or an elected official. Yet all of these happen in the real world. They don't happen with anywhere near the frequency the public believes. No consistent pattern of subjective or biased reporting exists except in a tiny minority of standard newspaper or radio or TV news operations. (Here we discount the supermarket tabloids and their ELVIS IS

ALIVE brand of "reporting.") No ten people in New York City dictate to all the U.S. media what will be reported. The media are diverse (although becoming less so as more and more newspapers, for example, become parts of groups or chains and as media converge with common ownership of newspapers, television, or radio stations and their joint websites).

Diversity is necessary. No thoughtful journalist will ever suggest one day's newspaper represents the total truth about what happened in the world the previous day. What that journalist will suggest, however, is that if the audience will read more than one newspaper, listen to radio newscasts, watch television newscasts (and not always the same station or network), surf the Internet or utilize news groups on the web, and buy *Time, Newsweek, The Economist,* or *U.S. News & World Report,* the truth will emerge.

IT'S NOT ABOUT BEING POPULAR

Surely, you must be thinking, in addition to all the other good things about journalism, the men and women who bring the nation its news and information are an admired species, attracting love and attention from an adoring audience. After all, information is essential in a democracy. Therefore, the bearers of this information must occupy a lofty position in society. Here we must disappoint you.

Journalists do *not* rate highly with the public. (In that regard, they are like some other institutions in the country: Congress and the Postal Service, for example.) Journalists often bring bad news. They report on wars and assassinations and corruption and fires and airplane crashes. Unable to do anything about the *message* in the media, some people get angry at the *media* themselves. Journalists can't react to this anger. Their job is to report the news. It's not their job to sugarcoat it. When the country went to war in the

Persian Gulf and journalists screamed over what they saw as unnecessary censorship by the military, most Americans sided against the press. Journalists were not seen as particularly valuable people in that war, and the country was in no mood to join them in efforts to pry information from the government.

So don't expect to be popular. A Gallup survey in July 2000 surveyed the American public to determine its level of confidence in various American institutions. At the top of the list was the military, with 64 percent giving it a ranking of "quite a lot" or "a great deal." Organized religion was number two (56 percent), followed by the U.S. Supreme Court and Banks (with 47 and 46 percent, respectively). Only 37 percent have "quite a lot" or "a great deal" of confidence in newspapers, with 38 percent having "some confidence." For television news, the numbers are about the same.

In yet another Gallup poll in 1999, respondents were asked to rank professions by "honesty and ethics." Journalists as a category came in as fortieth out of forty-five professions ranked, and were given "very high" or "high" marks totaling only 24 percent. Another 53 percent said they were "average" in their honesty and ethnics. (If you are curious, the top five professions considered the most honest by the American public in 1999 were, in order, nurses, pharmacists, veterinarians, medical doctors, and K-12 teachers. Almost traditionally, over several years of these surveys, car salespeople continue to be the worst rated of the forty-five jobs and occupations tested by Gallup.)

Another 1999 survey by the American Society of Newspaper Editors found that three of four Americans believe the media to be biased, particularly television news.

James E. Shelledy, editor of *The Salt Lake Tribune,* in a 1999 letter to the paper's readers discussing the ASNE survey on media credibility, however, responded to the bias criticisms of the public like this:

Let's start from ground zero: Every writer and every reader, if human, is biased. No story has ever been written or read objectively in the true sense of the word. Journalistic biases creep into stories when we choose words, when material is excluded or included, when we select sources, and when we place those stories in the newspaper. Each reader superimposes another set of biases on the prose. Genuine objectivity evades each end of the process.

That said, professional reporters and editors set aside emotions, philosophies, and the urge to propagandize when fashioning a news story. While it is humanly impossible to eradicate all biases, journalists can be fair in placing comments and facts in context and in presenting all sides of the issue. In other words, while true objectivity is impossible, fairness is attainable and ought to be the goal and hallmark of every good newspaper.

A somewhat older survey even showed the public thinking that there should be a law requiring newspapers to report equally on both major candidates in the presidential race. The people believe this despite the fact that such a law would be unconstitutional. Of course, newspapers *should* cover both candidates equally. But to *require* them to would violate the First Amendment to the Constitution, which guarantees freedom of the press (as well as other sacred liberties). And what would we do to editors whose newspapers didn't cover both candidates equally? Throw them in jail? Does that sound like a democratic nation?

So, if you decide to take the plunge and go into a mass media job, don't expect to be popular. As someone once put it, you'll be flogged by the public when you're right, and you'll be flogged by the public when you're wrong. You'll be criticized from the political left and from the political right.

But if you do the job right, if you follow the rules of accuracy and responsibility, if you serve the public and not yourself, you will have the inner satisfaction that comes with knowing your work is essential and that it serves, in the end, the cause of advancing democracy and its people. That's the true reward of journalism.

CHAPTER 2

JOURNALISM: 1690 TO THE PRESENT

A JOB THAT ENDURES

The journalist's job, it has been said, is to comfort the afflicted and afflict the comfortable. This oversimplified and overstated description of a complex craft contains a nugget of truth.

The statement suggests that conscientious journalists do their best to identify society's problems and help solve them with clear, accurate information. By focusing on problems and issues, journalists provide information the public needs to find solutions. If homelessness is a problem, journalists zero in on it. Some may spend a few days and nights living on the streets and reporting what it's like. Thus informed, the hope is, the public will do something. This is the "comfort the afflicted" part.

As for "afflicting the comfortable," what journalists mean is they keep a constant eye on all forms of government. If the government is lax, corrupt, or dishonest, journalists report it so that the public, mostly through the ballot box, will acquire better government. A fat cat public official, skimming public money for private use, has journalists to fear.

NEWSPAPERS IN COLONIAL AMERICA

It has always been that way in our country—even before there was a United States. In Colonial America, while we were still ruled by the British, journalists were busy comforting the afflicted and afflicting the comfortable. The American press was a partner to the American Revolution. The press exposed abuses by the British and fanned the flames of patriotism.

The Patriot papers weren't much like today's newspapers, of course. For one thing, they were openly partisan. If you wanted the other side of the story, you had to buy a newspaper loyal to the opposition. Today, ethical newspapers routinely print both sides of the news. They also may routinely run opposing points of view in their editorials or editorial columns, the only pages where opinions and taking a position are appropriate in today's media, unless the story is clearly labeled as such. The Patriot papers, on the other hand, planted the idea of revolution, and they encouraged rebellion.

The First Newspaper in America

Journalists in Colonial America were a particular target of the British Crown. That problem started with the very first newspaper in America. Printer Benjamin Harris published the newspaper and called it *Publick Occurrences Both Forreign and Domestick.* The newspaper appeared in 1690 in Boston. One story reported that "a day of Thanksgiving" had been established by the Indians. But another story was critical of the king of France. That was enough for the government. It stepped in. *Publick Occurrences* was killed after only one edition. The official reason was that the newspaper had no license to print.

The idea of licensing a newspaper sounds strange to us today, although in many countries the media still are controlled by their governments. Some members of the public do not understand this, but no one in the United States needs a license to print today. If you want to go to your home computer and create a newspaper and distribute it, you have every right to do so. You don't have to obtain anyone's permission, let alone buy a license. You are responsible for what you print, and if you libel someone, you may find yourself paying a great deal of money to that person. Still, you have the right to print.

In Colonial America, however, a license was required. The British Crown figured, and correctly so, that ideas were dangerous. So Harris's newspaper was killed.

The Boston Newsletter

Fourteen years passed before the Colonies again had a newspaper. The newspaper was John Campbell's *The Boston News-Letter,* and historians consider it the nation's first consecutively published newspaper. It first appeared in 1704 and had a monopoly in Boston for fifteen years. Underneath the newspaper's flag or nameplate (often incorrectly called its masthead), appeared the words, "Published by Authority." This meant Campbell was licensed and that the government approved his publication.

Campbell was loyal to the Crown so his newspaper was safe— as long as he remained loyal.

Anti-British Newspapers

Other newspapers began to appear. In 1721, the *New England Courant* appeared in Boston *without* the words "Published by Authority." The press had taken its first steps toward the great independence it enjoys today.

The Revolution was building steam. An event in 1735 stands out. John Peter Zenger ran *The New-York Weekly Journal.* It was a popular newspaper with the increasingly anti-British colonists. This made it *unpopular* with the British government, particularly Governor William Cosby. Cosby was a frequent target of the *Weekly Journal.* On November 17, 1734, Zenger was jailed, charged with seditious libel. In other words, he was charged with stirring up the people.

After months in jail, during which his wife Anna continued to print the paper, Zenger was brought to trial. In those days, all the government had to do was show that a seditious statement had been printed. It did not matter whether the criticism was true. In fact, the rule was "the greater the truth, the greater the libel." The government could easily turn aside a *false* criticism. It was the truth that hurt most. So if Zenger had printed what the government said he did, he would be guilty. At least that's what the government thought.

Zenger retained as his attorney Andrew Hamilton, considered by many the finest attorney in the Colonies even though he was then in his eighties. Hamilton readily conceded that Zenger had printed the stories the government said he had. To the government, the case had ended. But the government had underestimated Hamilton and Zenger—and the resistance in the Colonies to British rule. Hamilton told the court that if what Zenger printed was true then there could be no libel. For libel to occur, Hamilton argued, "the words themselves must be libelous—that is, false, malicious, and seditious—or else we are not guilty."

It took the jury only minutes to shout a verdict of "not guilty."

The trial not only gave a boost to the coming Revolution, but it helped establish a key legal principle still in effect today: Truth is a defense in libel. Libel must be false or it isn't libel.

By the time of the Revolution in 1775, thirty-seven newspapers were being printed in the Colonies. Most backed the Revolution.

FREEDOM OF THE PRESS

After the war, delegates to the Constitutional Convention in Philadelphia wrote the Constitution. When the framers of the Constitution, after meeting secretly, submitted it to the states for ratification, an outcry arose. The Constitution contained no reference to freedom of the press. Most state constitutions guaranteed that freedom. In 1791, the Bill of Rights—the first ten amendments to the Constitution—was ratified. The First Amendment guaranteed freedom of the press.

American journalists enjoy a unique freedom. The First Amendment reads, "Congress shall make no law...abridging freedom of speech, or of the press." Frustrated government officials occasionally try to clamp down on the nation's free press, but the press almost always wins in such confrontations. The First Amendment is hard to defy.

THE DEVELOPMENT OF MODERN NEWSPAPERS

After the war, and for the next two centuries, the nation grew rapidly, spreading from coast to coast. Hundreds of newspapers cropped up. Itinerant printers carried their clumsy typesetting equipment in wagons along with pioneers and settlers in the new lands. Even the smallest towns had newspapers, set by hand, one letter at a time. Soon the technology was to improve and with it the quality of newspapers.

Newspapers for the Working Class

In 1833, Benjamin Day founded the *New York Sun*. It was a revolutionary newspaper. Unlike its predecessors, the *Sun* was filled with news from the police beat and news about tragedies and natural disasters. It was written not for the intellectual elite but for the common person. And it sold for a penny.

The new working class created by the Industrial Revolution provided the *Sun* with a mass audience, which meant Day could attract more advertisers and charge them more for space in his paper. The formula is still in use today for all types of media. The greater the number of readers, listeners, viewers, or page "hits," the more the advertising costs.

James Gordon Bennett founded the *New York Morning Herald* two years later. His paper cost two cents, but it copied Day's formula about news and advertising and it, too, succeeded. Then Horace Greeley followed suit, creating the *New York Tribune* in 1841 and attracting an unheard-of circulation of 200,000.

In 1841, Henry Raymond founded *The New York Times*. Today it is widely viewed as the best newspaper in the country and perhaps in the world. But it was not until Adolph Ochs bought it in 1896 that it became a distinguished newspaper. Today its standards of fairness and accuracy are unsurpassed.

By 1910, after the Civil War and the invention of the telegraph, 2,600 daily newspapers were being published in the United States. Many cities had eight or ten newspapers. Today the country has about 1,700 daily newspapers and few but the largest cities have more than one.

Yellow Journalism

It could be said that this period, late in the nineteenth century and early in the twentieth, was journalism's adolescence. Journalism had not yet grown up. It was the era of "yellow journalism." The news was sensationalized and often fabricated. Hoax stories made their way into print, surrounded by doctored photographs, bogus scoops, screaming headlines, and endless promotions of the newspapers themselves.

Some people insist to this day that newspapers whipped up enthusiasm for war that resulted in luring the United States into what became known as the Spanish-American War. William Randolph Hearst, publisher of the *New York Journal,* and Joseph Pulitzer, publisher of the *New York World,* were the most notable of the yellow journalists and are most often named by those suggesting that the press led the nation into the Spanish-American War.

Muckraking

At this point magazines began to appear giving the newspapers competition. This may have led to the demise of yellow journalism. *McClure's, Collier's,* and the *Saturday Evening Post* showed up on newsstands and demonstrated a new kind of journalism: muckraking. The muckrakers went after corruption, exposing big oil and patent medicine frauds and combating child labor abuses. Many reforms resulted from this intense journalistic scrutiny.

Jazz Journalism

Yellow journalism was followed by Jazz Journalism, another name for the same irresponsible brand of anything-goes "reporting." A racy and largely inaccurate picture of the world was painted daily by journalists more interested in their own amusement than in providing information to their audience.

THE ELECTRONIC MEDIA

Radio

Then came radio and yet more competition. The first radio newscast occurred in 1916 and regular programming began in 1920. The National Broadcasting Company (NBC) was formed in

1926, the Columbia Broadcasting System (CBS) in 1927. The Mutual Broadcasting System was launched in 1934 and renamed the American Broadcasting Company (ABC) in 1945. Radio had a problem that the newspaper industry did not have. While one town could have ten newspapers—indeed, it could in theory have hundreds—the same was not true of radio. If radio broadcasts were not regulated, the airwaves would become a confused mass. Someone had to assign frequencies; someone had to keep the stations from bumping each other off the air. Since the airwaves are considered to be owned by society at large, the government stepped in. The Radio Act of 1927 was passed to keep the airwaves clear. The act created the Federal Radio Commission, forerunner to today's Federal Communications Commission, which regulates (not censors) both radio and television.

Today, Americans own something like 470 million radios. The stations number 4,700 on the AM band and 3,400 on FM. Radio's significance today, however, pales in comparison to television.

Television

The first television newscast was in 1940. Most of the country first began purchasing televisions in the late 1940s and early 1950s. A national love affair with the tube began.

Today, a majority of Americans say they receive most of their news from watching television. Most journalists, including most television journalists, are upset by this. While some television news shows are excellent, (*60 Minutes* comes to mind), television news remains largely a headline service. A thirty-minute newscast contains about as many words, not counting commercials, as there are in *one* column in a newspaper. Clearly, a citizen who relies exclusively on television for news will be underinformed. Some politicians know this, and they run for public office on flimsy issues designed more to attract TV "sound bites" (often as short as ten seconds) than public debate on the real issues.

Today, American news and information media constitute a huge, high-tech industry bombarding us constantly with messages. These independent, constitutionally protected journalists play a pivotal role in society. While perhaps not as powerful as some people believe (the press cannot mold or manipulate your mind), the press certainly sets our national agenda. Journalists say, "We don't tell you what to think. But we do tell you what to think about." If it's on the front page of the paper, the lead story on the 11:00 P.M. news, a key story on the radio, or an item flashing across your computer screen on your favorite Internet news site, it will be the talk of the town the next day.

Technology

The Internet began to develop in the late 1960s, as scientists at research institutions all over the world constructed independent computer networks that could convey information in the event of a nuclear holocaust. The net came into popular use in the early 1990s as a public communication medium, when commercial services such as CompuServe, Prodigy, and America Online made it accessible to anyone with a computer and a modem. Computer programs like Microsoft Internet Explorer and Netscape Navigator made surfing the net not only popular but downright simple.

Journalists found that by using the Internet they could gather information from a broad range of sources faster than ever before. The public discovered the same thing. As a result, the lines of media began to blur in light of the Internet. Organizations that once relied exclusively on print, like *The New York Times, The Los Angeles Times,* or *The Denver Post* to reach their audience, now enhance their written stories by posting video and audio bites on their websites. Similarly, broadcast media now must rely heavily on copy to capture the attention of surfers to their sites.

Although the Internet began as an exceptional research tool for journalists, it has developed into an incredible employer of them. Small and large news services now operate some kind of net-based component. News organizations, whether broadcast or print, break stories on multimedia websites often before they run on the nightly news or in the morning edition. When the news of Lady Diana's car accident broke, many people found the story on the web before the first network "Special Report" ran.

Public relations also has changed in the wake of the World Wide Web. Organizations of all kinds use the Internet to bolster their public relations campaigns, offering cut-and-paste press releases and streaming video and audio sound bites at the click of a button to site visitors. Such organizations also hire journalists to manage Internet messaging and positioning for their E-business divisions.

Exciting advances in technology are providing new opportunities for journalists and communications professionals, and though the media are changing, the basic skills of the journalist remain the same.

ETHICAL STANDARDS FOR JOURNALISTS

What guides journalists? Certainly not the law. The media enjoy almost unlimited freedom to print whatever they see fit, provided it is not libelous. Instead, journalists are guided by their ethical standards, which often are formalized into codes of ethics. Following is the Society of Professional Journalists' Code of Ethics.

Code of the Society of Professional Journalists

PREAMBLE

Members of the Society of Professional Journalists believe that public enlightenment is the forerunner of justice and the foundation of democracy. The duty of the journalist is to further those ends by seeking truth and providing a fair and comprehensive account of events and issues. Conscientious journalists from all media and specialties strive to serve the public with thoroughness and honesty. Professional integrity is the cornerstone of a journalist's credibility.

Members of the Society share a dedication to ethical behavior and adopt this code to declare the Society's principles and standards of practice.

SEEK TRUTH AND REPORT IT

Journalists should be honest, fair and courageous in gathering, reporting and interpreting information. Journalists should:

- Test the accuracy of information from all sources and exercise care to avoid inadvertent error. Deliberate distortion is never permissible.
- Diligently seek out subjects of news stories to give them the opportunity to respond to allegations of wrongdoing.
- Identify sources whenever feasible. The public is entitled to as much information as possible on sources' reliability.

Sigma Delta Chi's first Code of Ethics was borrowed from the American Society of Newspaper Editors in 1926. In 1973, Sigma Delta Chi wrote its own code, which was revised in 1984 and 1987. The present version of the Society of Professional Journalists' Code of Ethics was adopted in September 1996.

- Always question sources' motives before promising anonymity. Clarify conditions attached to any promise made in exchange for information. Keep promises.
- Make certain that headlines, news teases and promotional material, photos, video, audio, graphics, sound bites and quotations do not misrepresent. They should not oversimplify or highlight incidents out of context.
- Never distort the content of news photos or video. Image enhancement for technical clarity is always permissible. Label montages and photo illustrations.
- Avoid misleading re-enactments or staged new events. If re-enactment is necessary to tell a story, label it.
- Avoid undercover or other surreptitious methods of gathering information except when traditional open methods will not yield information vital to the public. Use of such methods should be explained as part of the story.
- Never plagiarize.
- Tell the story of the diversity and magnitude of the human experience boldly, even when it is unpopular to do so.
- Examine their own cultural values and avoid imposing those values on others.
- Avoid stereotyping by race, gender, age, religion, ethnicity, geography, sexual orientation, disability, physical appearance or social status.
- Support the open exchange of views, even views they find repugnant.
- Give voice to the voiceless; official and unofficial sources of information can be equally valid.
- Distinguish between advocacy and news reporting. Analysis and commentary should be labeled and not misrepresent fact or context.
- Distinguish news from advertising and shun hybrids that blur the lines between the two.

- Recognize a special obligation to ensure that the public's business is conducted in the open and that government records are open to inspection.

MINIMIZE HARM

Ethical journalists treat sources, subjects and colleagues as human beings deserving of respect. Journalists should:

- Show compassion for those who may be affected adversely by news coverage. Use special sensitivity when dealing with children and inexperienced sources or subjects.
- Be sensitive when seeking or using interviews or photographs of those affected by tragedy or grief.
- Recognize that gathering and reporting information may cause harm or discomfort. Pursuit of the news is not a license for arrogance.
- Recognize that private people have a greater right to control information about themselves than do public officials and others who seek power, influence or attention. Only an overriding public need can justify intrusion into anyone's privacy.
- Show good taste. Avoid pandering to lurid curiosity.
- Be cautious about identifying juvenile suspects or victims of sex crimes.
- Be judicious about naming criminal suspects before the formal filing of charges.
- Balance a criminal suspect's fair trial rights with the public's right to be informed.

ACT INDEPENDENTLY

Journalists should be free of obligation to any interest other than the public's right to know. Journalists should:

- Avoid conflicts of interest, real or perceived.

- Remain free of associations and activities that may compromise integrity or damage credibility.
- Refuse gifts, favors, fees, free travel and special treatment, and shun secondary employment, political involvement, public office and service in community organizations if they compromise journalistic integrity.
- Disclose unavoidable conflicts.
- Be vigilant and courageous about holding those with power accountable.
- Deny favored treatment to advertisers and special interests and resist their pressure to influence news coverage.
- Be wary of sources offering information for favors or money; avoid bidding for news.

BE ACCOUNTABLE

Journalists are accountable to their readers, listeners, viewers and each other. Journalists should:

- Clarify and explain news coverage and invite dialogue with the public over journalistic conduct.
- Encourage the public to voice grievances against the news media.
- Admit mistakes and correct them promptly.
- Expose unethical practices of journalists and the news media.
- Abide by the same high standards to which they hold others.

Unlike the codes that guide doctors or lawyers, journalists' codes have no teeth. An unethical lawyer can be disbarred. An unethical doctor can lose his/her license. An unethical journalist can (and will) be fired. But he or she can't be penalized by the state for ethical misconduct. Nor can he or she lose a license. It would be unconstitutional for a journalist to have to have a license. The most severe punishment for an unethical journalist is that he or she may not ever find work in the field again.

JOURNALISTS' FUNCTIONS

We expect journalists to provide clear, accurate, unbiased information. For the most part, they do just that, often against great odds (such as hostile sources or uncaring audiences). How then can we judge how well they do? Journalists have roles assigned them, informally, in our society. By knowing these roles and monitoring their work, it's possible for an informed citizen to determine how well a journalist is doing.

The Political Function

Perhaps the most important job assigned to the press is to monitor the activities of government. This is called the political function. The press calls it its watchdog role. The First Amendment is in place to guarantee that the press is able to perform this function. A press fearful of government would not make much of a watchdog. Freedom of the press is there so our system of checks and balances will work. The press has no higher duty.

The Entertainment Function

Life is not all city council meetings and politics. We also expect the press to entertain us. That's why *Larry King Live,* "Dear Abby," and the comic strips are there. The political function is far more important to society than the entertainment function, but most journalists concede that government news often can be dull.

So if your morning paper or evening newscast makes you smile, that's the entertainment function at work.

The Social Function

The press has a social function, too. What we talk about, what we think about during a day are apt to have come to us from the media. The old small-town America of backyard, barber-shop, and around-the-crackerbarrel conversation is long gone. Now, yesterday's headlines are today's conversations, and they fuel a lot of E-mail communications.

The Economic Function

The press also has an economic function, which is fulfilled through advertising and news of business products and services, and the stock markets. The nation needs healthy mass media to keep its economic wheels turning.

The Record-Keeping Function

And the press keeps records for us: Who is born, who dies, who gets married, who gets divorced, what the president said yesterday or today, who won the big game, and so on. The record-keeping function, though hardly glamorous or dramatic, is an important one.

THE HISTORY OF CANADIAN JOURNALISM

Journalism in Canada developed later than it did in Great Britain or the United States. Vast distances, a harsh climate, rugged terrain, and a sparse population initially limited the spread of the printing press. Yet, these factors made the development of the news media a pressing necessity to Canada during the years it built itself as a nation.

Canada's First Papers

No printing presses were allowed in New France because the Bourbon monarchy feared that their output could not be controlled. But in the British colony of Nova Scotia, Bartholomew Green and John Bushell, two Boston printers, imported the first printing press and started the Halifax *Gazette* in 1752.

Almost immediately after the British conquest, American printers brought presses into Quebec. The bilingual Quebec *Gazette* was founded in 1764 by two Philadelphia printers. In 1778, the Montreal *Gazette du Commerce et Litteraire*, was founded by Fleury Mesplet, a protege of Benjamin Franklin, in a failed attempt to persuade the French-speaking population to join the American Revolution. Later on, the *Gazette* became solely an English-language publication and today vies with the Hartford *Courant* as the oldest continuously published newspaper in North America. This pioneer press did not make any waves as it was largely under the thumb of the British Crown.

The end of the War of 1812 spurred development, immigration, and the growth of newspapers. A more feisty, opinionated press appeared. Journalists debated the form of British rule, asking the public to decide for or against "responsible government." How much power should the British-appointed governor have as opposed to democratically elected assemblies? Journalists assumed a more prominent position in society. They even led the failed rebellions of 1837 against British rule.

In French Canada, a press arose to assert the rights of French speakers and to prevent their assimilation into the English-speaking population. Here, too, we see the beginnings of the popular perception that the newspaper press had a civic function—providing a public forum for different political opinions.

Canada had its own freedom-of-the-press judicial case similar to the Peter Zenger trial in the United States, only about a century later. In 1835, Joseph Howe, the editor of the *Novascotian*, published an anonymous letter accusing the governor of corruption. The British Crown charged Howe with seditious libel, a treasonous offense. Howe successfully defended himself, establishing the Canadian precedent of truth being a defense against libel and also the right of a jury to determine guilt or innocence. Howe's example furthered the popular idea of the newspaper as a defender of the rights of people against arbitrary government authority.

A Changing News Emphasis

Canada's underdevelopment and proximity to the United States led to a taste for American publishing products. A Canadian publishing industry including books and magazines did not develop fully until the twentieth century. However, only a local press could provide social and commercial information. Thus, economic and population growth in the 1840s and 1850s led to the emergence of a daily press in Montreal, Toronto, and smaller cities.

This news press was extremely partisan. By 1857, party politics dominated the debate about the nature of independence from Britain. Virtually every one of the 291 newspapers allied themselves with a favored political party. Not only editorials but news stories openly championed party causes. When the party won power, allied newspapers benefited from the patronage of government printing and advertising contracts.

After Confederation in 1867, partisan politics still filled the news pages. Only now, the papers debated the type of government for the new Dominion. For many, the editorializing of newspapers led to popular ideas about the news press having a public function.

Yet, as Canada industrialized, change was coming to the newspaper publishing world. George Brown, the founder of the Toronto *Globe*, was a transitional figure in the development of a more business-oriented and thus independent news press. Although a prominent partisan politician, his newspaper became required reading even for people who hated his political views.

Constant innovations at the *Globe* meant that it printed more news faster than its competitors. It was the first to use a powered press, the telegraph, and other technological developments. Brown successfully gambled that investments in new technical developments and more features and reporters would provide the greater circulation resulting in more advertising revenue.

By the 1870s, a new breed of newspaper publisher, such as Hugh Graham (Montreal *Star*) and John Ross Robertson (Toronto *Telegram*), founded newspapers modeled on the American "Penny Press." Partisan politics gave way to a greater emphasis on local news—crime, scandal, and corruption—often reporting it in a sensational manner. Entertainment began to accompany the informative and persuasive purpose of news reporting.

Changing the news emphasis forced publishers to pay as much attention to the bottom line as to editorial content. The features and technological innovations and increasingly specialized journalists necessary to persuade more people to buy a newspaper were expensive as the price per edition dropped significantly. This meant that advertising edged out subscriptions to provide the revenues for the mounting expenses of running a newspaper.

The content of newspapers became more diverse. To capture different groups of readers, newspapers added more features, including serialized novels, science columns, sports news, women's pages, and comics. All this foreshadowed today's bulky omnibus editions.

Regulating the Media in Canada

By 1900, the Canadian newspaper world was a lively place where even small cities had several competing papers. But newspaper readership was saturated, so competition grew fierce. Helped by the postal service and railroads, newspaper publishers invaded other locales.

Other competitive techniques were used. The Southam family began Canada's first chain of newspapers. First expanding from Hamilton to Ottawa near the turn of the century, the family added another three dailies in the West by 1911.

World War I caused more consolidation and concentration in the newspaper industry. The overall number of newspapers dropped from a high of 138 French and English dailies to a low of 90 in 1940.

This situation improved somewhat with the postwar boom. The Southam chain continued to expand. Other chains formed to meet the challenge, such as the Federated Press and the Thomson organization. The number of single newspaper cities rose, and the number of independent dailies fell to only a handful today.

The issue of concentration and the decrease of independent editorial voices worried the public. In 1970, the government established the Special Senate Committee on the Mass Media, better known as the Davey Committee, to look into the question. It concluded that "diverse and antagonistic sources" of information, central to free and open debate, was threatened. However, its recommendations to halt concentration were never carried out.

Ten years later, a new round of consolidation caused the government to set up the Royal Commission on Newspapers to study the implications of the newspaper industry being in increasingly fewer hands. None of its recommendations to safeguard a diversity of opinion were acted on either.

The Canadian government has historically been more active in regulating and developing the communications media than has the U.S. government. Canada's communications systems were essential to the nation-building of the last century and national unity today. That is why government policy prevents foreign ownership of the newspaper industry.

Radio is another good example. Already in 1905 the government regulated the airwaves for security reasons. Following the pioneer broadcasting of Pittsburgh's KDKA, Montreal's CFCF began programming in 1920. The success of America's newly formed radio networks, NBC and CBS, enticed Canada's biggest radio stations to join them in 1930. Canadian nationalists feared that American programming would soon squeeze out Canadian content and pressured the government to act.

The government responded with the first of many national commissions on the mass media. Following the recommendations of the Aird Commission, the government set up the publicly funded Canadian Broadcasting Corporation (CBC) in 1936. Its mission was to preserve and encourage Canadian cultural expression. Although similar to Britain's BBC, the CBC was different in that privately owned radio stations were allowed to co-exist with it.

Television provides another example of government involvement. Again, fears of being swamped by American content prompted the government to fund a national TV network in 1950. But by the end of the decade, many Canadians were dissatisfied with the CBC's monopoly. They desired access to the American broadcasting that one-quarter of the population enjoyed. In 1958, the government allowed competitive stations, which in turn formed private networks, the English CTV and the French TVA. Much of their programming is American in origin.

Initially, the CBC regulated the airwaves. But after complaints from private broadcasters, the government set up an independent body, eventually called the Canadian Radio-Television Commission (CRTC). This commission sets the standards for Canadian broadcasting.

Perhaps the most important and certainly the most controversial of these standards concerned the amount of foreign (read American) programming that Canadian radio and TV stations could broadcast. In 1960, Canadian content was set at 60 percent. This encouraged Canadian journalism because radio and TV broadcasters, especially those who depended on American programming, could meet their content quotas through news programming.

Yet, problems arose with content quotas. Broadcasting American programs was extremely profitable from an advertising standpoint. Gradually, the CBC, which did not carry advertising, suffered especially with government funding cutbacks. Today it carries advertising and also transmits American programs. For many Canadians, this development means a reversal of the CBC's original mission.

The need for Canadian content also extended to magazines. The Canadian editions of *Reader's Digest* and *Time* magazines were the country's most profitable periodical advertising vehicles. In 1975, the government ended the tax advantages of these publications. This allowed the monthly *Maclean's Magazine* to become Canada's first weekly newsmagazine in 1978.

Canada's News Media Today

Today, the Canadian news media is in flux. Despite the gloom-and-doom of the concentration prognosticators, journalistic career opportunities have actually increased. Even the venerable newspaper industry has openings. About twenty years ago, a rival tabloid chain started so that many cities have a *Sun* to compete with the regular daily. Satellite-publishing allowed the *Globe and Mail* to become Canada's national daily. In 1998, the competing Hollinger chain created the *National Post* to become Canada's second national daily.

This rivalry benefited journalists. The *Globe and Mail* beefed up its reporting, features, and special editions while the *National Post* created new positions and offered higher salaries to entice talented journalists. In addition, the spread of the giveaway "alternative press" in many cities and the free subway newspapers in Toronto and Montreal have created opportunities for young journalists who need journalistic experience.

There are 118 daily newspapers in Canada (111 English), 1,025 community papers (815 English), 551 radio stations (439 English) and 118 TV stations (81 English). Convergence is occurring. The media scene has been likened to an information highway: Newspapers are the shoulder, TV the slow lane, and the Internet the passing lane.

Vast cross-media and information conglomerates have been forming. For example, North America's largest printer, Quebecor, also controls large English and French tabloid chains, other broadcasting outlets, as well as half of Canadian Online Explorer (www.canoe.com), an on-line news server. The other owner is Canada's largest telecommunications firm and Internet provider, BCE, which has just taken over the CTV television network.

CanWest Global Communications, an electronic media broadcaster took over Hollinger Publications (which swallowed the Southam Newspaper chain) to enhance its cable TV outlets and its Global TV News channel. Most of its big cities dailies have on-line portals.

If you are interested in a career in Canadian journalism, there are many helpful sites to browse for more information. For Canadian-based publications on-line, including E-zines and on-line news services (www.cs.cmu-edu); Canadian Newspaper Association (www.cna-ac.ca/); Canadian Community Newspapers Association (www.ccna.ca); Canadian Association of Broadcasters (www.cab-acr.ca/); and the Radio and Television News Directors Association (www.rtndacanada.com/).

The History of Canadian Journalism was written by Minko Sotiron, who teaches history of journalism at Concordia University and history at John Abbott College in Montreal, Canada. He is the author of *From Politics to Profit: The Commercialization of Canadian Daily Newspapers, 1890–1920* (1997) and *An Annotated Bibliography of Works on Daily Newspapers in Canada, 1914–1983* (1987).

CHAPTER 3

WRITING: THE KEY TO ALL JOURNALISM CAREERS

Walk into any journalism classroom on the first day of the semester and you'll hear the teacher saying something like this:

> Journalists are hard-working and tenacious. They don't take no for an answer. They don't quit until the job is finished. They're curious. They're creative. They enjoy people and care about them. They're well-informed on current events.

The list could go on. What the teacher is trying to do is identify the characteristics of journalists. This probably is a waste of time.

Journalists are like everybody else. They come in all varieties. Many are outgoing, but you can be shy and be a journalist. Many are assertive, but you can be low-key and be a journalist. Many are tough, but you can be a softie and be a journalist. No one should reject journalism as a career because he or she doesn't fit some old movie's stereotype of what journalists are like. The best advice still is "be yourself."

But successful journalists do share one trait. All of them can write. It is the fundamental skill, whether you want to go into newspapers or magazines, print or broadcast, web-based sites, public relations, or advertising. Someone writes every broadcast, every story, every headline or caption, every news release, every

Internet entry, and every advertisement. The ability to craft clear, powerful sentences is required of all journalists, no matter what part of the business they're in. So don't spend your time in English class daydreaming about conquering the world of journalism. You'll need the writing skills your English teacher is showing you.

Some journalists are virtual geniuses with the language. Most are not. Most are skilled craftspeople who have trained their eyes and ears to recognize bad writing and to punch the delete key. (We used to say good writers have big wastebaskets. Now we say good writers wear out the delete key zapping the bad sentences.)

Some journalists struggle with writing, of course. The business is full of stories about great reporters who couldn't write a word. Some of those stories are true. But every year sees fewer and fewer poor writers succeeding in journalism. Jobs are scarce, and the people doing the hiring are choosy.

"So where does that leave me?" we can imagine many readers asking. "I get C's in my English classes, spend three times as long on essays and term papers as my classmates, and still get my papers back covered with red ink. And spelling? It's beyond me. When I trust spell check, it misses little typos that are spelled correctly but are still the wrong word, like 'that' for 'than' or 'there' for 'their.' English is a hard language!"

SPELLING—A SIXTH SENSE?

This statement raises many issues. Let's take spelling first. Some people are blessed with almost a sixth sense about spelling. They're able to spell a word correctly the first time they hear it. This ability appears to be genetic. Others are less fortunate. They can do math but not words. They're great mechanics but don't ask them how to spell "accommodate." They can't do it. And our spelling whiz probably can't change a tire.

Learning theorists, however, reject this thinking. Everyone can learn how to change a tire. And everyone can learn how to spell. Many people simply memorize the words, a few at a time, the way spelling used to be taught in the lower grades. Others undertake formal study of the rules of English. "I before E except after C" is still a good rule to know. And there are many others, of course. (Is it "cemet*a*ry" or "cemet*e*ry?" Remember that everyone in the cemetery is at ease, and think of "ease" as E's. It's all E's. Ceme*te*ry.) The best thing someone with spelling problems can do, however, is wear out two dictionaries a year looking up words. It's no crime to be a poor speller. It *is* a crime not to get into the dictionary habit of looking up words. If you're working on a computer, make sure you have a spell-checking program, and run it on everything you write. But, don't put blind faith in it. There is no substitute for carefully reading your copy. The spelling problem can be solved.

A LEARNABLE SKILL

What about the other problems facing our imaginary writer? All those C's in English and all those hours working on essays only to have them covered with red ink? Talent plays a role here, of course. Just as some people have good spelling genes, so do some have good writing genes. In the movie *Amadeus,* Wolfgang Amadeus Mozart had talent, and the music he wrote came effortlessly. His hapless rival, Antonio Salieri, had to work harder and the music wasn't as good. *But it wasn't bad, either.* And today music stores sell Salieri's works as well as Mozart's.

Hard work and perseverance can go a long way toward overcoming lack of natural talent. The words may not flow for you the way they do for the Mozart at the next desk. But that doesn't make everyone else's words unimportant. Just harder. Yes, English is a difficult language, but it's not impossible to master.

One way to improve your writing ability is by reading, and not just newspapers or magazines either. Read the back of the cereal box at breakfast. Read the signs on the bus on the way to school. Always have a novel going. Carry it with you and read a paragraph whenever you have a spare moment. Haunt the library. Read books *about* writing. And read and memorize what all those remarks in red ink are about!

No one denies that writing is hard work. To be sure, there are days when the words flow and your fingers dance over the keys magically. Such days are to be treasured because for most of us they come rarely.

The Writing Process

Most people would rather do anything than get started writing. Watch them sometime. A typical journalism student comes back to the newsroom or classroom after a reporting assignment and a ritual begins. First something to drink. Then a chat with a friend. Then maybe the computer keys need brushing off. Or the screen needs to be cleaned. Finally, it's time to write. And nothing comes out. Somebody once said writing is easy, "You just stare at the screen until blood appears on your forehead."

When it's time to write, the thing to do is write. Get started. You'll probably throw out the first three or four paragraphs you write while your mind's warming up. That's fine. Hit the delete key. Once you're under way, it almost always gets easier. And when you're done, the rewards are great. The author of *The Seven C's of Writing* offers the following reassurances:

> At the end you never know that what you've done is the best you can do. Nor do you know for certain that the reader is going to read what you've written. But there's a thrill that

comes from seeing your handiwork in print that more than compensates for the turmoil and the struggle. Then it dawns on you that by golly you've done *something*. By having the strength, tenacity, and courage to display your abilities and your convictions, you've reached, affected, and motivated hundreds, perhaps thousands, of your fellow human beings. (*The Seven C's of Writing*)

Writing is, at least in part, a collection of tricks. Perhaps things like rhythm and color and beauty are difficult to attain except for literary Mozarts. Yet, some of what constitutes good writing is simple and learnable. Anyone can master tight writing.

Tight Writing

Every editing book contains long lists like this short one intended to introduce the notion of editing for tightness. Don't write bouquet of flowers. Just write bouquet. Don't write made arrangements. Write arranged. Don't write made a decision. Write decided. Don't write Easter Sunday. Easter is always on Sunday. Don't write Jewish rabbi. All rabbis are Jewish. Don't write due to the fact that. Write because. Don't write new recruit. All recruits are new. Just write recruits. Can you detect the wordiness in "present incumbent," "rough estimate," "basic fundamentals"? Of course. Anyone can learn it.

Grammar and Usage

The rules of grammar and usage are written down and learnable. Nouns and pronouns have to agree. Subjects and verbs have to agree. Some of it is tricky. Most of it is not. If you're interested in journalism, you must be interested in language. This is fundamental and will not change no matter what new technology appears. Computers don't write; people do.

Many journalists are word freaks who derive great joy out of unusual words or word combinations. Many headline writers are punsters. Many a game of Scrabble has been played around newsroom copydesks late at night after the newspaper is finished. If you want into journalism, get into words. Care and precision in language are not out of your reach. Remember that "farther" and "further" are different words with different meanings. Note that "anxious" and "eager" are not interchangeable. Do not call the man being married the groom. A groom cares for horses. The man at the altar is the bridegroom.

Even people with bad writing genes can learn the difference between "affect" and "effect," "principle" and "principal," "libel" and "liable," "guerrilla" and "gorilla," "capital" and "capitol." Your spell-checking program will sail right past those words because the way they're spelled is all right (there is no such word as "alright"). So you'll have to know the difference.

Knowing the words on this small list is not a huge accomplishment. Filling your head with dozens and dozens of these types of distinctions, however, is a big step on the road to good writing. And you don't have to be a Mozart to be able to do it.

No one has ever been forced to use a cliche. No one *has* to use jargon or fuzzy language. No one is compelled to write long, unwieldy sentences. Euphemisms can be avoided. All of these enemies of good writing can be recognized and axed. No mystery here. Just common sense.

In an essay, Clarke Stallworth of the *Birmingham (Ala.) News* once made this common-sense observation:

> Good writing is clear. Bad writing is not.
>
> That's the big difference between the two. Why is the difference so important?
>
> To begin with, clear writing holds the reader. The reader's eye moves along the line of familiar, friendly words, cruising smoothly across the page. No breaks, no potholes, and

the reader concentrates on the message. And the golden spark of communication arcs between writer and reader.

If the writing is clear, the writer can use a whole arsenal of good writing techniques—he or she can make pictures, tell stories, use lively verbs, slice out jargon and unnecessary words and cliches, put people in the story, show rather than tell.

Later he added this guideline:

Put the 10-20-30 yardstick on the writing. If your average paragraph is 30 words or less, you're probably OK. If your average sentence is 20 or below, you're probably in the ball game. And if your percentage of big words is less than 10 percent (5 percent is better), then you're in the writing business.

The principles are easy to state and easy to follow. Use short words, short sentences, short paragraphs. Spell the words right. Follow the rules of grammar. Avoid cliches, jargon, fancy words, and euphemisms. Edit carefully; few written efforts are perfect on the first try. Read widely. Try to write every day.

Benjamin Bradlee, former executive editor of the *Washington Post,* was talking about reporters when he said the following. His words apply as well to everyone considering a career in journalism:

The best reporters are those who combine energy, judgment, curiosity, fairness, skepticism, commitment and knowledge with the ability to express themselves with grace and clarity.

CHAPTER 4

THE NATURE OF NEWSPAPER WORK

The word "variety" springs to mind in describing the work of newspaper journalists. So much goes into creating a newspaper that people with all types of talents can find a place there. Reporters, writers, headline writers, artists, page designers, editors, and specialists of many kinds are needed.

Further, newspapers vary so much in how often they come out, what audiences they serve, and what their circulations are that there's no correct way to lump them under the one term "newspaper." Newspapers offer a variety of jobs in a variety of circumstances.

The usual, generic concept of "newspaper" is that of a daily product that tries to cover, first a city, then a state, then the nation, then the world. The United States has about seventeen hundred daily newspapers that generally do just that.

But they vary, too. Some have many editions a day and a blockbuster edition on Sunday. Some papers come out five times a week plus Sunday, usually skipping the Saturday edition. Some publish five times a week and take the weekend off. And more than five thousand newspapers come out on a nondaily basis, that is, once, twice, or even three times a week. In addition, all of the larger papers and many smaller ones have websites that require constant updating.

Some newspapers, no matter how often they come out, ignore the general news completely, aiming their information at specialized audiences. These audiences might be senior citizens or members of a religious group. They might be campers, exercise enthusiasts or collectors. "Newspaper" is a rich term. That aside, in some respects newspapers are all alike. At least the processes they use are alike. Someone assigns the stories, reporters gather and write the stories, editors check the stories for errors, someone decides on pictures or artwork, someone creates a page layout, someone writes the headlines and captions. This is as true at the weekly *Dawson County Herald* in Lexington, Nebraska, as it is at the huge metropolitan daily *Philadelphia Inquirer.* The processes vary little.

Someone even said all newspapers *smell* alike, a not unpleasant mixture of ink, paper, photographic chemicals—and sweat.

REPORTERS

In examining what people at newspapers do, reporters come first because they're the eyes and ears of the newspaper and the people it serves. No newspaper is any better than its reporting staff. Great photographs, great headlines, great layouts...all amount to little if the reporting isn't there. Looking at it another way, if the reporting *is* there, the photographs, headlines, and layouts are still secondary—important, yes, but less important than the information found by reporters.

At a weekly newspaper, reporters often also are photographers, illustrating their own stories. Then they may switch hats and edit the copy, write the headlines, and create the layout. They may even find themselves helping with production, preparing page layouts on the computer, selecting and importing art and photographs, and determining the use of color. At the smallest papers, the reporter might even help distribute the paper or sell paperclips at the counter.

Many ranking newspaper editors prefer reporters who began their careers at small papers, not necessarily nondaily papers, but at papers where everybody does a little of everything. It's dangerous to specialize too early. Some time on the police beat and some time covering education, sports, or the courts can be valuable in providing the groundwork for general reporting. Reporters who start at a larger paper may never come to understand the entire process, but instead learn only about their small corner of the newsroom. Reporters at a small paper absorb even the financial aspects of newspaper publishing. Most reporters probably prefer to remain aloof from newspaper economics, but that's a luxury. In these bottom-line days, everyone needs to know about money.

Many types of reporters ply their trade at newspapers. Many are specialists, covering business or the judicial system. Some specialize in international coverage, business, religion, technology, or minority affairs. Such reporters generally are free of the responsibility of covering breaking news: the airplane crash, the fire, or the surprise news conference. Most set their own assignments. In an ideal situation, they tell the editors what they're working on rather than the other way around.

General Assignment Reporters

General assignment reporters (GA's) come to work every day not knowing for sure what they're going to be doing. They're sent where they're needed. One day they might attend an announcement of this week's lottery winners. The next day they might find themselves doing a story about the construction causing traffic jams downtown. And the following day they might interview the winner of the local spelling bee. They're generalists, and they have to be able to produce good copy rapidly.

Beat Reporters

Beat reporters cover the same agencies or subject-matter areas all the time. Typical beats are police, schools or education, courthouse, business, statehouse, the legislature, the governor's office, and science and medicine. Beat reporters deal with the same sources day after day and must develop relationships with them. They have to demonstrate a track record of accuracy and fairness to their sources or they can be cut off. If they develop that record, then sources will open up to them, provide tips, and offer copies of reports and documents. Beat reporters whose sources don't trust them can't be effective. Winning this trust requires considerable people skills.

One danger, if reporters stay on the same beat too long, is that they can begin to *think* like their sources, or write like them. There's nothing worse than an education writer whose stories start sounding like interoffice memos at the local university. It's possible for beat reporters to get too close to their sources, to develop friendships that can interfere with news judgment, such as when a source/friend becomes the object of criticism.

Some Washington, DC, reporters, it is said, have been known to start *dressing* in the same manner as the U.S. senators they cover—dark suits, power ties, the little half glasses like those Senator Edward Kennedy wears. Many newspapers rotate beat reporters every once in a while to avoid these problems.

Beat reporters, incidentally, also usually make their own assignments; they know better about what's happening on their beats than their editors do.

Lifestyle Reporters

Lifestyle or feature reporters are a blend of many talents. Rather than working out of the city desk on hard-news material, they specialize in writing about trends, consumer issues, food, books, entertainment, and restaurants, and the whole array of material newspapers present that doesn't fit as hard news.

Such writers are usually free to explore different writing styles, to "featurize" their work. And they live on off-beat ideas. Hard-news journalists sometimes look down on the feature section, asking feature writers as they walk past the city desk, "Hey, you working on a late-breaking recipe today?" Feature writers' work is much approved by the audience, however. And there is no question that today's newspapers, for better or worse, are placing more emphasis on feature stories than they did in the past. As newspaper circulation declines, editors search for a formula that will help them win back readers—and to do this they often look to the soft news.

Investigative Reporters

A few larger newspapers have investigative reporters or investigative teams. They work on longer projects, sometimes spending as much as a year on one story or series of related stories. Often they work in secret, with only senior editors aware of their projects. They tend to write exposes and to uncover wrongdoing or corruption. They also became investigative reporters after long years as general assignment or beat reporters.

Investigative reporters spend a great deal of time poring over records in musty courthouses, searching through on-line websites, chasing down telephone records, and filing Freedom of Information Act requests with the government to pry loose information the government would rather not give out. Being an investigative reporter can be tedious work. But it pays off in benefits to society when a wrong is righted—and it pays off in prizes that can enhance a newspaper's reputation.

Sports Reporters

Sports reporters do much the same thing as their counterparts in features or on beats. Most newspapers divide the various athletic endeavors of their town or region and assign a reporter to each. Someone covers university teams, several handle local high schools, and senior reporters cover the professional teams. Beginning sportswriters tend to cover high schools—or even bowling or outdoor sports.

Interestingly, it can be harder to cover high schools than major college or professional sports. Sportswriters covering high school have to keep their own statistics and cover the games as well. At a pro or big-college game, the writers can concentrate on the game. Representatives of the teams or schools bring the statistics—not to mention the coffee—to the pressbox and even provide photocopied quotes from coaches and players if the writers don't have time for post-game interviews.

Sportswriting poses the same dangers beat reporting does: Sportswriters can get too close to their teams. They can become cheerleaders, advocates of the team, instead of advocates of good information *about* the teams.

Some of the best writers on most newspapers are in the sports department, often unfairly called the toy shop by the hard-nosed, hard-news citizens at the city desk.

A large amount of every reporter's time is spent on the telephone. A reporter trying to do two stories at once has to work the telephone—quite a skill in itself—and stay close to it. Run out to a source's office, and you might miss three important calls while you were away. Reporters use many techniques, but mostly they call and call, ask and ask, verify and verify. They read documents, attend meetings, attend news briefings—and always they wait for sources to return calls. Perseverance and patience are good qualities for any reporter.

COPY EDITORS

Reporters and copy editors make up the two largest groups of people at most newspapers. They complement each other even if they don't always compliment each other. The two need to work together although tensions often arise between them. Reporters don't like seeing their copy changed. Copy editors have their own opinions about how stories should be presented. Nonetheless, *wise* reporters know how often top-notch copy editors save them embarrassment and correct inaccuracies; thus they treasure the good editors.

A description of a copy editor's work will make it sound almost clerical or routine. It's anything but. Copy editors are essential to the production of good newspapers.

After a reporter writes a story, a city editor or an assistant city editor looks at it, depending on the size of the newspaper. Then the story goes to the copy desk. At smaller newspapers, there may be no one between the reporter and the copy desk. At the copy desk, the head of the desk will look over the story and assign it to a copy editor.

Copy editors do many things with the story. They check it for spelling, grammar, and punctuation. They check it for style, that is, they see that it conforms with the newspaper's stylebook. (The stylebook is a set of rules requiring that certain words or concepts be expressed the same way by everyone on the staff. A newspaper can't write "adviser" in one paragraph and "advisor" in the next, even though both are correct spellings. The stylebook dictates which to use.) Copy editors check a story for organization: Is the lead (the most important news) in the seventh paragraph? If so, the copy editor may ask the story's reporter to rewrite it. (Here's where the tension can come in.) If that's not possible, the copy editor may rewrite it, or send it back to the city desk for the revision.

Copy editors watch for libel, poor taste, inaccuracies, unclear sentences, misspelled names of people or streets or buildings, wordiness, cliches, and jargon.

If a copy editor misses something, it almost certainly will end up printed in the paper. Production staffers who used to catch the errors of journalists in the back shop have largely been eliminated by technology. So there is no backup for the journalists. That's why this work definitely isn't clerical.

When copy editors finish editing a story, they then have to perform a crucial task. Copy editors write the headlines. (On a small paper, of course, reporters might write their own heads. But on a paper of any size at all, copy editors do this.) Headline writing is a job that requires speed, great word skills, imagination, and precision.

Copy editors have to condense the main points of a story in an attractive and eye-catching way and into as few as three or four or five words. It's not easy. Good headline writers are considered invaluable in any newsroom.

Like reporters and all newspaper employees, copy editors do their work at computer terminals. The days of pencil and paper and messy glue are, thankfully, gone. Computer technology has placed new pressure on the copy desk. Some tasks once done in the composing room by printers are now done at the copy desk.

Thus, the best place for a new journalism school graduate looking for work is on the copy desk. That's where some of the great jobs are. Make sure it's for you, however. Copy desk work requires people with top-notch language skills and an eye for detail. The hours tend to be more regular than those reporters work. They may be *odd* hours, though. Some copy editors start work at 2:00 A.M. Others come in at 6:00 A.M. Some start at 5:30 in the afternoon. Generally, though, they work eight hours and go home—even if they're driving home at 3:00 A.M.

LAYOUT AND PAGE DESIGNERS

Layout and page design staffers are the newspaper's visual people. They create pages that are attractive and easy to read. Working on their own or under the direction of an editor, page designers decide where on a page to place the various elements—photos, artwork, charts or graphs, and stories.

This isn't just mechanical work. It's journalism. What message are we sending our readers by putting one story at the top of the page and another at the bottom? What balance can we achieve, both graphically and journalistically, by mixing state and local news or by placing related stories together?

Techniques in newspaper design are improving and so is the technology these journalists use. Encouraged by *USA Today* and technology that has made layout more cost-effective, most newspapers are putting new emphasis on color, and this challenges page designers to use it creatively. Staff artists usually work closely with the page-design staff, creating graphics, charts, and maps, under deadline, on their own computers.

EDITORS

Depending on the size of the paper, one editor may run the whole show. Or there may be twenty people with "editor" as part of their title. Editors are bosses. They set policy. Some set policy and stand back and watch. Others set policy and then roll up their sleeves and help carry it out (a practice that doesn't always please the staff).

At most newspapers, the top-ranking journalist is known as the managing editor, although executive editor is a fairly common title, too. The managing editor decides what the paper is going to be about, sitting in on news meetings, suggesting some stories, and vetoing others. He or she (usually he, frankly, but we're working on it), does most of the hiring and firing and generally sets the tone for the paper.

The managing editor may have several assistant managing editors or he or she may have none. The assistant managing editors usually have a specific territory to watch over, such as graphics or features, for example.

The city editor directs the local reporting staff. He or she has to juggle dozens of stories, answer staff questions constantly, make instant news decisions, and help guide the overall philosophy of the paper. The city editor is like a general in a battle. Where should we send our forces? How big is this story and can we get a reporter there in time to cover it? The city editor sits on a hot seat between reporters and higher-ranking editors and sometimes feels great pressure from both. Many reporters aspire to be city editor; it's a prestigious job. But it's a hard one that doesn't permit much relaxing at work.

Most papers have a news editor. When all the managing editors and assistant managing editors are gone, the news editor gets the paper out, making news, coverage, and layout decisions by the minute. This person is on the spot and must be able to react quickly to changing news situations.

If ranking editors decide in a meeting at 5:00 P.M. what will be in the paper the next day, the news editor—who will be there at 11:00 P.M. when a plane crashes—has to be able to fit the new situation with the 5:00 P.M. decisions. If you like to be in charge, if you like deadline pressure...this is the best job at any newspaper.

COLUMNISTS

A lucky few people get to write their own columns, to express their opinions under their bylines every day or every week. Some people consider this a premium job. Others cringe at the idea of having to produce a signed, inventive, readable, and thoughtful piece on a regular—sometimes daily—basis.

Columnists, no matter how many columns they may be ahead, talk about how they're always nagged by the next column they must produce. You see them wandering around the newsroom, reading, talking—anything to get an idea.

Some of the most widely read items in any newspaper are columns. Some of the highest paid people in any newspaper are columnists. They have tremendous influence and some personalities— like Larry King—become nationally famous, with columns in *USA Today,* and live interview shows on CNN.

Journalistic beginners would be advised, however, to get a strong education, learn the basics, and make their way up the ladder before turning to columns. There's a long line ahead of you.

EDITORIAL CARTOONISTS

Editorial cartoonists are a special breed of people. They not only have to be artists; they have to be journalists and critics, too. An editorial cartoonist who is merely a good artist but who has nothing to say won't go far. Nor will someone who is a great social critic but can't draw.

College newspapers are a great place to cut your teeth if editorial cartooning is what you'd like to do. Most college newspapers would like good, locally produced cartoons. Most have no such thing available.

If this is your interest, prepare five or six cartoons on local subjects and go see the editor. As for a course of study, get your academic adviser to explore a combination of art, political science, business, and journalism.

EDITORIAL WRITERS

Editorial writers are like columnists in a way. They have to produce all the time, on the creative days as well as on the dry ones. The one difference is that editorial writers usually are anonymous. What they write represents the paper's viewpoint, not necessarily their own, which can be a problem. Sometimes editorial writers believe one thing and have to write another, although larger newspaper have staffs big enough that this usually can be avoided.

Most editorial writers were once reporters or editors who opted for editorial writing because they have something to say and the skills to say it well. They need to be good researchers and, yes, good reporters. Some editorial writers just read stories, look at the ceiling, and then comment. The best ones, however, do their reporting by making phone calls and checking old files, looking at a lot of information on the Internet, and generally getting first-hand information before offering opinions.

PHOTOGRAPHERS

Photographers are visual people. But their work entails more than just setting the camera, focusing, and shooting a picture. Like communications itself, photography is undergoing significant changes caused by the digital world. Although there is still a technical side to photography, and although many photographers still are able to work with film and chemicals to develop their photographs in the darkroom, digital cameras are rapidly becoming the norm. Many photographers today are adept not only at taking the quality photo that will be on the front page tomorrow, but at taking short video clips at the same time that will be quickly downloaded onto the newspaper's website for a breaking story. This area alone will continue to undergo significant change as photographic equipment evolves in the new technology, serving print media as well as video and web-based media.

Regardless of how technology affects photographers, photo-journalists have to be a mix of technician and journalist. They have to know what will move the hearts and minds of those who see their photos. They have to know how to take an event or situation and capture its essence in such a way that it enhances the public's understanding of it. They cannot be people who only take pictures. All media photographers have to be reporters. There is nothing as discouraging or embarrassing as a reporter who when asked by an editor for the names of people in a photo cannot provide them. A photographer who is a reporter will have that type of information—the two together make the story, not just the photo alone.

CHAPTER 5

CAREERS IN ELECTRONIC MEDIA

In addition to offering music, entertainment, and advertising, radio, television, and the Internet offer the journalist excellent career alternatives in broadcast news.

Over a half-billion radios are in operation today in the United States and Canada, receiving signals from more than nine thousand AM and FM radio stations. Nearly all households in America have at least one television set. More than two thousand television stations send us news and information. Hundreds of special interest media also exist to serve special audiences—educational, religious, minorities. In addition, nearly seven thousand cable television systems offer a variety of local, news, and special-interest channels throughout the nation.

More and more Americans, perhaps the majority, rely on electronic media for daily news, sports, and information about the events and issues shaping their lives. The electronic media, through increasingly effective technology, bring today's news and events to us as they happen, anywhere in the world.

REQUIREMENTS FOR A BROADCASTING CAREER

Writing Skill

The most critical skill in handling radio and television news is the same as in other journalism careers—writing. Learning the basic skills for newswriting will prepare you for adapting those skills to the special needs of the broadcast media. Read the lead story in today's newspaper. Then watch that story on television. The newspaper is not as constrained by time. The stories are longer, offer more insights and depth, go behind the scenes to provide detailed reports by observers, and provide background information important to understanding the implications of the story. Broadcast media, however, have only a few minutes—sometimes seconds—to tell the story, unless the broadcast is a news special. Aided by visual material on TV, you see the event as it is described by the reporter on the scene or in the television newsroom. On the radio you hear an even more brief report of the event, often including comments from participants.

Clarity in broadcast copy becomes even more critical. The key at that point—and something that could determine your success as a broadcast journalist—is what *not* to include in the story. Television newscasts seldom contain more than fifteen minutes of news, yet it is arguably where most busy people get their news. In those fifteen minutes, newscasters have to tell you everything that happened around the world and around your town. What's more, as broadcast journalists move from one market to a larger one, they are required to tell more and more in less and less time. Even videotaped stories that reporters have worked on all day or perhaps for days, as a rule of thumb, seldom receive more than thirty to ninety seconds of air time within a newscast. (There are news channels that do have more time to cover stories, particularly breaking news. But most stick to a format of short segments that are repeated frequently.)

That's why clarity in writing is critical from the start. Short, descriptive, well-constructed sentences are the rule. Not only can the listener follow the story more clearly, the announcer can say the words more clearly.

But the journalists' job in all three media—newspaper, radio, and television—is the same: to report the story accurately, fairly, and as completely as possible within the format and time limitations of the specific medium. You work equally hard to uncover the news story for your audience.

Experience

Not unlike applying for most jobs, your personal presentation, appearance, and personality will play a dominant role in getting hired. Next to writing skills, experience is critical. Internships will place you ahead of those without such experience. Most radio and television stations offer internships, many of which are paid.

You may want to find part-time jobs at local broadcast media while in high school and throughout college. Don't overlook the student radio and television stations and educational broadcast media as laboratories for real world experience. These jobs don't necessarily have to be in the news department. Any media job helps you learn how the business functions and what reporters do, and gives you a clearer understanding of the craft. You also get your foot in the door so that you can be considered for other jobs as they become available.

Education

In a study of radio and television news directors, more than 70 percent of the electronic media surveyed indicated that a four-year undergraduate education is either absolutely essential or important to a broadcast career. News directors surveyed strongly (70 percent) rate a journalism/communications degree important in evaluating candidates for jobs. About 20 percent ranked graduate degrees as important to a broadcast career.

Survey respondents said among the jobs available for graduating college students in broadcasting, 32 percent were in the newsrooms. Don't be unrealistic about the first job in broadcast journalism. Beginning salaries are not high, usually starting at $20,000 to $25,000, depending on the size of the market and station. Advancement may be slow and turnover in the top jobs infrequent, especially in television.

RADIO CAREERS

Products of modern technology, such as tape recorders, cell phones, and radios, help the radio journalist bring you the sounds of events as they happen or record them for use on regular newscasts. Live reports from a fire or hazardous waste spill, reports from a news conference or the locker room after a major sports event, and interviews with people making today's news all come from the radio journalist.

The number of jobs in radio news will depend on the size of the station and the community it serves. Many small stations may have only a few journalists to compile the day's news from extensive wire services, the Internet, and audio news networks providing summaries of events from around the world and on special topics, such as business, agriculture, the weather, entertainment, and sports. Larger stations may have specialists who report news in these and other areas. Stations that specialize in providing all news all day will draw from many sources—staff, radio broadcast services, websites, and wire services.

News Director

The news director organizes and plans the day's coverage. If the station has news reporters, they're assigned by the director to cover events of the day and to prepare other special news reports. In smaller stations, the news director often writes and edits the news as well as delivers the newscast.

Larger radio stations have editors who compile the news from a variety of sources. Individuals specializing in sports, farm news, business news, entertainment news, or other specialized topics prepare information for the newscaster to deliver on-air, or prepare taped or live reports themselves for use in newscasts or at specific broadcast times.

JOBS IN TELEVISION NEWS

Similarly, television newsrooms are served by a variety of wire services and video networks. We have all become familiar with the leading U.S. and Canadian national television networks—ABC, CBS, NBC, CNN, Bloomberg, MSNBC, CBC, CTV, and Fox. But we also have seen an increase in recent years in the variety and length of local news coverage in many communities. Local stations hire staff in the capitol to "feed" (report, videotape a presentation, and send it by satellite to the local station) the story for use in tonight's news. Trucks are equipped with satellite transmission capabilities that, when linked with camera equipment virtually anywhere, can bring live reports from the scene of an airline crash that may have occurred only minutes ago; the site of a shuttle launch; or a state parade or a postgame celebration. We see police invade crack houses and share the emotion of a presidential inauguration. Technology makes it possible for us to be a part of today's news as it happens, or to see it as it happened within only a few minutes.

News Director

Television jobs are increasing in number in many communities where there is a growing emphasis on news. The TV news director is responsible for managing the news operations. Staff is hired and fired, reporters assigned to stories, editors directed in preparation of video stories, camera operation organized, and news and sportscasts scripted under the eye of the news director. News directors usually have worked their way through the ranks, serving several years as reporters, editors, or newscasters. Some come through newspaper careers or after years in radio news. They are ultimately responsible for what we see and hear on television news programs.

Larger stations may have managing editors to assist the news director. A managing editor supervises the daily operations, while executing the plans outlined by the news director.

Producers and Directors

Producers and directors (sometimes one person has both titles) put the news show together. These people bring the video from the scene of the news together with the newscaster; they also make sure that slides, charts, graphs, or other visual material are ready and in the proper order. They are responsible for the product we actually see and hear during the allocated time period. Larger stations will have assistants in these areas who may work on segments of the newscast.

Reporters

Television reporters have to be quick on their feet. They spend a lot of time digging into stories, interviewing sources, and working with editors. Many television reporters deliver the news on the air personally. Others provide information and material for the newscaster to deliver. And in many TV news situations, reporters have little time to get the information accurately and as completely and fairly as possible so that it can go on the air as it happens, "live from the scene."

Newscasters

Newscasters are more well known to us than most reporters. These "anchors," as they have become known, are personalities with whom viewers become familiar. Viewers develop loyalties to specific news programs because they feel more comfortable with the newscaster, placing confidence in the news being delivered. These anchors include individuals who handle sports news and meteorologists who handle the weather.

Anchors, contrary to some viewpoints, are not just "pretty faces" who read the news. Most anchors are journalists who have worked hard as reporters and editors to get to their positions, which are premium jobs in television.

Specialists

Like newspapers, television news programs have specialists who investigate, write, edit, and report news in such areas as education, health, entertainment, science, agriculture, and government, to name a few. People in these jobs usually have special education or backgrounds in these subjects that they have acquired over time. They also have worked their way through the ranks from beginning reporter. They also may come from years covering a beat for a newspaper.

Photographers and Graphic Artists

Photography is a critical element for television. It is a visual medium. Photojournalists do more than point a camera and work with a sound person to record the events. They have creativity that allows them to attract attention by capturing the emotions and feelings that are part of the news, too. In some communities, photojournalists may also write, edit, and report the news. In other communities, they work with a team of people to produce the story.

At most television stations, photographers also are technicians. They set up microwave links from mobile trucks, for example.

Graphics are an equally important part of most television news operations. Artists work with computer graphics systems to create still and animated art and generate the names and titles that are seen on the screen during newscasts.

The Work of Many

There is another job that is often not thought about. The archivist keeps track of all tapes and stories so that they can easily be updated when new developments occur, sometimes many months later.

It takes a lot of other people to produce television programs, such as camera operators, technical directors, make-up staff, and sound technicians. When they aren't working on news, they are involved in other program activities of the station.

Regardless of the specific job an individual holds in either radio or television, broadcasting, like other media, requires teamwork. The anchor would be useless without news directors, managers, editors, reporters, camera and audio operators, switchers, floor directors, film and video editors, photojournalists, news specialists, sportscasters, set designers, staging and lighting experts, the worldwide news wire and video networks, and a wide range of support staff, financial and administrative personnel, and management. Broadcasting journalism offers challenge and excitement to the individual willing to work hard.

CHAPTER 6

MAGAZINE AND NEWSLETTER JOURNALISM CAREERS

Journalists can find plenty of challenging, exciting, and rewarding jobs working for magazines and newsletters. Thousands of magazines and newsletters are sold at newsstands, through subscriptions, or through the mail. With computer technology, more and more magazines and newsletters appear on-line at home, school, or office for those who have a simple telephone hook-up. Many of these electronic versions are free; others require subscriptions.

FEATURES OF MAGAZINES AND NEWSLETTERS

One feature of this type of journalism is that many magazines and newsletters appeal to your special interests, hobbies, or other career areas. For example, you could work for a magazine for education professionals, combining an interest in education (or maybe even a teaching degree) with your journalistic skills. Or you could work for a magazine covering stories of interest about stamps, cats, orchids, religion, politics, restaurants, your city or state, farming, bluegrass music, investing, interior design, sewing, or one of hundreds of other subjects.

In addition to working on the major weekly news magazines (or sometimes special newspapers) that cover news events from around the world and maintain staffs or bureaus in key cities, many career opportunities exist for top-notch writers, editors, and photojournalists. In fact, it is estimated that more than twenty thousand magazines circulate in the United States alone. There are even magazines about magazines! Hundreds of new periodicals are started each year—and hundreds fold each year, too.

Think of the magazines you read. Why do you read them? They provide you with general news and information, or they provide you with information about an area of special interest. If they stop keeping you interested, you will stop buying them and shop for others.

To be successful, a periodical must understand the interests and information needs of its readers. As those interests change, the publication must change. Readers expect their magazines to be on the cutting edge for new information—a leadership role—in providing news. If they fail to change or lead, they can lose readers. Losing readers affects the amount of money for which advertising can be sold and could end the publication's life.

ORGANIZATION OF MAGAZINES AND NEWSLETTERS

There are probably as many ways to draw organization charts for magazines and newsletters as there are publications. Smaller ones may have only two or three full-time employees, buying articles from freelance writers or news services.

Freelance writers are common in the magazine and newsletter business. A freelancer is often self-employed and may write for a variety of publications. Or a freelancer combines writing with another career or interest—a doctor who writes for medical magazines, or a teacher who writes for education publications, for example. Stories a freelancer writes are sold to an appropriate publication. You could even be freelancing right now—writing articles about topics of special interest to you. (Check out *The Writer's Handbook,* published by The Writer, Inc. It is a guide to publications, telling you what types of stories they buy and how to sell to them.)

Publisher

At the top of most periodical organization charts is a publisher—the person responsible for all departments of the publication, such as advertising, promotion, marketing and sales, circulation, and editorial. This job may be filled by someone who has a strong background in business or advertising, or someone who has worked his or her way up through the editorial department. The publisher also could be the magazine's owner.

Editor

An editor, or editor-in-chief, leads the editorial side of the publication that, depending again on size and scope, may be organized into subject or topical departments, in turn headed by department editors. The publication may have a staff of writers and editors, use a group of reliable freelancers, or obtain articles from freelancers who "shop" for publications to buy their work.

Regardless of the organizational structure and layers—or lack of layers—content is king. Magazines may offer a great opportunity for a career in journalism. And, like other careers, any journalism experience you can obtain through part-time jobs, internships, and formal college education is important. But with the variety of opportunities, individuals who have excellent backgrounds in a particular subject can take "crash" courses that will help them sharpen their writing skills for periodicals. Some of the courses are taught during summers, over weekends, or at night. Some courses are part of continuing education programs or correspondence classes. It also is important not to forget that freelance writing can be done throughout another career—combining two or more important interests.

CHAPTER 7

JOURNALISM AND PUBLIC RELATIONS CAREERS

As in magazines and newsletters, there are thousands of opportunities for you to combine an interest and ability in journalism with other areas of interest for a career in public relations.

WHERE PR PROFESSIONALS WORK

Today, public relations professionals work for school systems; colleges and universities; doctors and medical clinics; hospitals; governmental, social, and community organizations; businesses; industry; dot.coms; professional associations and clubs; and politicians and entertainers, to name a few.

Within the broad term *public relations* are specialty areas for careers, such as working with news media; coordinating community relations; writing, editing, and managing newsletters, magazines, and other publications for an organization; handling broadcast/video communications—scriptwriting, editing, production, and distribution; measuring public opinion; handling relationships with governmental officials—lobbying and public affairs; consumer relations; investor relations; marketing communications; issues management; speech writing; and managing special events.

Public relations is a process of communications designed to build support, understanding, goodwill, and morale for a business, a person, a product, or an institution. A public relations professional develops a strategy that uses an array of communications techniques.

REQUIREMENTS FOR PR WORKERS

Public relations professionals often come from news media backgrounds or graduate from colleges and universities offering journalism/public relations degrees or programs.

Writing is the most important and critical skill required for effective public relations careers. Also important are:

- the ability to develop effective strategies to use an array of communications tools and techniques to accomplish your organization's objectives;
- the ability to manage a number of activities effectively at one time;
- the high quality of your personal communication and speaking skills;
- a strong knowledge of business and/or of the particular organization for which you work.

There is no better training for a career in public relations than working for a newspaper. You will learn to sharpen your writing skills for a general readership. You'll be well prepared to ask hard questions and know how to do your homework for your readers. You will work under the pressure of deadlines.

In a public relations job you will need to be able to write effectively, translating complex or difficult information into terms an average person will understand; in other words, to bridge the communications gap between your organization and one or more members of its audience.

Accuracy, credibility, and integrity are essential to being a successful public relations person. While you represent a point of view held by the organization you work for, media and others will respect you if you are a credible source. Be candid. Don't hide the bad news.

Include business courses in your undergraduate education. Most public relations jobs require a general understanding of business. Many professionals recommend a dual major or suggest that if you have an undergraduate degree in journalism, you also obtain a master's degree in business. Many journalism graduates believe that their entire future will be working for the media. But far more journalism graduates may switch to public relations than remain with the media. And, a background in business will be important for you to get the better jobs. Remember, journalists seldom write about journalism or public relations. You write about, or represent, the activities of businesses, organizations, and institutions.

CHAPTER 8

SUPPORTING CAREERS IN JOURNALISM

Some people like the excitement of the news media, but they don't want to be writers, editors, or photographers. There are other careers that can be rewarding in media.

ADVERTISING

For example, it takes money to publish a newspaper, magazine, or newsletter; operate a broadcasting station; maintain a public relations agency or department within an organization; or keep websites current. Each of these organizations has advertising departments that sell, create, and provide advertising services. Without advertising, we would pay very high prices for the media we enjoy. This book isn't intended to discuss advertising opportunities, but there are many helpful books on the subject, including *Careers in Advertising,* also published by VGM Career Books.

OFFICE SUPPORT

There are many support positions within the office including administrative assistants, accountants, bookkeepers, and librarians (archivists). Someone has to coordinate and hire staff, manage the personnel functions, and administer the payroll, benefits, and retirement programs of the organization; these people usually come from a human resources or finance background.

MARKETING

There are also staff members who provide marketing services and promotional activities for the media. Consider the outdoor billboards, bus posters you see all around you, the news and advertisements you hear on the radio, and the print publications promoting a particular series of investigative reports or local newscasts or programs you watch on television stations. And media conduct their own programs for public relations benefits, such as crime stopper efforts, health fairs, food and clothing drives for the needy, concerts, and other community service projects. Public relations and advertising are important and necessary jobs within many media businesses. The media would not survive without readers, listeners, and viewers.

TECHNOLOGISTS

Today's media rely heavily on technology and the people proficient in its use. Media employ computer operators and programmers, experts on satellite technology, and operators of sophisticated computer graphics equipment for such diverse uses as preparation of colorful page layouts, advertising, weather shows, simulations for news features, charts, and internal business reports.

Webmasters have become essential players in all media and business. Webmasters utilize a variety of skills including graphic design, writing, and programming technology. Whether establishing or maintaining an organization's presence on the Internet, the webmaster's competence and creativity are key to the way the organization is viewed by visitors to its site. Journalistic skills become very important, as key messages must be put forth in a clear and concise manner, grabbing a maximum audience while using limited space.

Printers today operate precision machines that run much like computers, delivering just the right amount of various colors of ink to the pages you see.

CIRCULATION

And someone has to see that you buy and receive the products. Circulation of printed publications must take place throughout a wide market area. In the case of national newspapers and magazines, there may be regional printing facilities with vast trucking and mail networks to see that you get today's paper today.

With the rapid growth of cable television services has come a network of sales personnel, installers, and related business functions.

The news media are businesses. There are a lot of jobs that need to be filled by qualified men and women in order for the journalists to deliver their written products to the reader, listener, and viewer. If writing isn't your key interest, you can still have a rewarding career working with the media. It's exciting to be where the action is, helping people keep informed, entertained, educated, thinking. Helping stimulate the economy. Helping to keep government under public scrutiny. And, yes, helping shape the future by fairly and accurately delivering today's news to the public.

CHAPTER 9

PREPARING FOR A JOURNALISM CAREER

Let's say you've made your decision. You want to become a journalist.

You know the work is both rewarding and demanding. You know about the commitment you'll have to make. Still, you've decided journalism is for you.

Now what? How do you prepare for a journalism career?

PATHS TO SUCCESS

There's no easy answer, no one way to do it. Many paths can lead you to journalistic success.

A College Education

A question certain to come up early as you ponder what to do next concerns college. Is a college education required for a journalism career? Well, no, it's not *required* in the sense that a lawyer has to pass the bar exam or in the sense that a pharmacist has to pass state exams to be licensed.

Many successful journalists passed up college and started their careers armed only with a high school diploma. Notice the past tense here. The journalists just described tend to be older, and they began their careers in a different era. Today, however, there is no question: If you want to be a journalist, go to college. Examples of exceptions are too rare to count much in making your decision.

Journalism Degree vs. Liberal Arts

The next question is more complex. Is a journalism degree necessary for a journalism career? Journalists, journalism professors, editors, and station managers disagree widely. Here are the arguments.

Those who believe a journalism degree is *not* necessary argue that what a journalist needs most is a broad, liberal education. They say the study of history, economics, law, English, foreign languages, political science—the whole range of a liberal education—is more important than studying journalism.

The tricks of the journalistic trade, the argument goes, can be taught easily on the job. Journalism classes are a waste of time. Every journalism class taken is a history class *not* taken. Every minute spent working on a school newspaper is a minute *not* spent studying Shakespeare. Besides that, they argue, too many journalism professors are failed journalists who retreated to the campus because they couldn't make it in the "real world."

People who believe this advice would be journalists who avoid journalism school and concentrate on becoming Renaissance men or women, truly well-educated people who can work effectively no matter what the subject matter of a story might be.

The other side of the story goes this way. To toss off journalism classes as merely passing along "tricks of the trade" is oversimplified. Journalism involves more than a few "tricks" that can be taught haphazardly in the newsroom, where there is little time for teaching anyway.

Journalism schools offer courses in mass media law, history, ethics, and the role of the press in society. At its best, journalism education creates not just journalists but thoughtful journalists. It's not enough merely to know how to write a story. A journalist must know why the story is being written (and sometimes when it's best *not* to write a story). Few working editors in a newsroom have time to coach young writers on the intricacies of newswriting, let alone law or ethics. The argument that you can learn journalism on the job is flawed because there is so little time on the job for teaching. It's true that the basics of newswriting, interviewing, and copyediting can be learned as you go. Still, there's much to be said for systematic learning. Journalism 201 follows Journalism 101 at a university. And where does the would-be journalist who never studied journalism learn press law? After the libel suit is filed?

As for journalism professors being failed journalists, who would deny that there's some truth to this? It's not so much "failed" as it is burnt-out. Indeed, some journalism profs teach because they got tired of the hard work of journalism, or of the odd hours or low pay. The majority, however, teach by choice, teach because teaching gives them joy and an opportunity to serve students and their craft. The best journalism professors have never *really* left journalism.

In the argument between journalism education and liberal arts, there's truth on both sides. One of the authors of this book worked five summers as adviser and writing instructor to a group of young journalists brought to Arizona for a journalism fellowship. They were all just out of college. Each was assigned a job at a newspaper but also learned through speakers, seminars, classes, and individual writing instruction. Participants in the program came from all sorts of educational backgrounds. Some were from small liberal arts schools. A few had Ivy League educations. Many came from important university journalism programs. A handful were picked from lesser-known journalism programs.

In assessing their performance, only one important pattern emerged. Successful participants were well-educated, whether it was in journalism or not. The ones with "J-schools" in their backgrounds knew the terminology better and got off to faster starts. But what really mattered was the quality of their education. And a good education can be found at hundreds of universities.

If you decide to pursue a college education in journalism, you still must decide on which college to attend. They're not all alike. In some ways, the arguments about journalism school vs. liberal arts are based on a false premise. There is no contradiction between going to a journalism school and getting a liberal education, provided you're careful about what school you pick and how you go about getting your education.

Accredited and Unaccredited Programs

If you pick an accredited university journalism program, you'll be *required* to concentrate on the liberal arts as well. The organization that accredits journalism schools insists that journalism majors take no more than one-fourth of their total credit hours in journalism. Thus, three-fourths must be devoted to liberal arts.

Some unaccredited journalism programs permit students to take a third or more of their units in journalism. Such programs do, indeed, undercut the notion of a liberal education. With all those units in journalism, what are you going to write about that you'll understand? Suppose you cover a speech and the speaker talks about supply-side economics. You took no economics courses because you were too busy taking every journalism class in the catalog, and your story makes no sense.

But even at an accredited school you can graduate basically uneducated if you do it wrong. Every journalism professor knows the pitfalls. If all you do in college is journalism, you're passing up much of your real education. (See Appendix C for a list of accredited college and university programs.)

Getting Good Grades

Many journalism students overdo it. They devote all their time to their journalism classes or, more likely, to the school newspaper. They skip English classes, go infrequently to economics classes, pick the easiest foreign language and barely pass it. They graduate with a 2.1 grade point average (GPA) and wonder why they can't find a job.

School newspapers can provide wonderful experience for a journalism student, but not at the price of a 2.1 GPA.

Do grades count? Lots of people go through life with their 2.1 GPAs and never pay any penalties. Others graduate with 3.8 GPAs and never feel like they're rewarded for their effort. These are exceptions. Grades *do* count.

They count when the faculty votes on scholarships, when editors weigh the job applications of two otherwise equal candidates with widely varying GPAs. They count when it's time to pass out honors and awards and when it's time to decide who gets into prestigious academic honorary societies. And they count if you want to go to graduate school.

Graduate School

Probably, if you're just now thinking about college, graduate school seems like a million miles away and something you haven't thought about anyway. Someday you might. What if you want to teach at the university level, for example? You'll need advanced degrees, and you won't be able to get into graduate school without the grades. Most graduate schools require at least a 3.0, and many put the standard much higher than that.

More and more journalists are coming into the newsroom with master's degrees. A few even have Ph.D.'s. Law degrees are becoming more common, especially for people covering the judicial system.

Here most journalists agree: Advanced degrees are fine, especially if they add a specialty on top of a journalism degree. Many people, however, advise against getting *two* journalism degrees. If your undergraduate degree is in journalism, find a specialty to study in graduate school. If you have a liberal education from your undergraduate days, a master's in journalism might provide just the right amount of journalism schooling.

Picking a College

Picking a college can be difficult. Make sure you touch all the bases. Visit a guidance counselor. Request the college catalogs. Write the alumni association for graduates in your area and interview them.

If at all possible, however, your strategy should include a campus visit. You can learn a great deal about a journalism program by such a visit. For one thing, you can get an idea of how the journalism department feels about students just by seeing how you're treated. Are you made to feel welcome? Is a faculty adviser available to see you?

Visit the school newspaper. If you want the *real* story about a journalism program, ask the students, not just the professors.

Make sure you find out the school's strengths and weaknesses. Some journalism schools put most of their effort and money into broadcasting. This would be no place for you if you want to go into print journalism. The reverse also is true. Steer clear of print-emphasis programs if your interests are in broadcasting.

OTHER LEARNING OPPORTUNITIES

Your quest to prepare yourself for a journalism career should include some other elements. Visit your local newspaper, broadcast station, or public relations firm. Ask the women and men there for advice. Most people are generous with their time when a young person wants advice. It's flattering for journalists to talk to someone who wants to be what they are. Ask these journalists how they prepared themselves. You'll find an array of paths.

In the meantime, become a student of journalism in your private world. Read newspapers, all you can get your hands on. Forget the tapes in your car: On the way to school or work, listen to National Public Radio. Watch a variety of TV newscasts and evaluate them. Make it a habit to read a variety of magazines. Surf the web and examine news, government, and corporate sites. Go to your library and find the section on journalism.

Camp there.

CHAPTER 10

IS TEACHING FOR YOU?

Many people who wish to become journalists have other interests as well. A typical one, especially for someone just finishing high school, is teaching. After years of classroom work watching teachers in action, many young people develop an interest in teaching. This should not be discouraged at all.

Teaching is a rewarding life, but it's not without problems, of course. It is just that these problems aren't always readily visible to a student. Like professional journalists, teachers work long hours under sometimes difficult circumstances. Pay, too, is low, but as we said earlier, it is wrong to measure the satisfaction in a job by pay alone.

To see a student struggle with this decision for weeks and then to see the joy that comes when they've realized that teaching is for them—well, money has nothing to do with that sort of reward.

But experienced teachers of today will tell you their jobs are becoming more difficult. You may have seen the surveys. Fifty years ago, teachers said their biggest problems had to do with students talking or chewing gum in class or sneaking a cigarette in the rest rooms between classes. These problems seem pretty tame compared to what teachers face today. Drugs and alcohol, broken homes, pregnancies, school violence…today's students often face severe problems—and they bring them into the classroom.

Do you have what it takes to become a teacher? The qualities of successful teachers are many, but most people would agree that the really good ones share certain traits. Number one, perhaps, is empathy, the ability to place yourself in another person's position and, therefore, understand that person. Good teachers have to be tough, of course, to maintain discipline and order in the classroom. But warmth, good humor, and patience are every bit as important as toughness.

If you want a career in teaching, you must prepare for it. In college, you will need a dual specialty. You need to take a journalism program as well as a teacher-preparation program through the teacher's college or the education department. You have to learn both to teach and what to teach.

In journalism, you probably ought to specialize in the news-editorial area, or print, in other words. Most schools still put more emphasis on the school newspaper than on broadcasting. You will need layout skills, not only for the newspaper but for the yearbook as well. Many journalism teachers advise both publications.

In addition, be aware of the fact that most teachers, particularly at high schools, don't have the luxury of specializing in just one subject. In addition to journalism, you will need a specialty in some other area. Many journalism teachers also teach English. Assignments in history, social studies, or government are common.

Somewhere along the way in college, try to pick up some professional experience. Internships or part-time media jobs are important. Nothing enhances a teacher's credibility with students more than having real-world experience. It is one thing to teach from the book. It is quite another, and quite better, to teach from experience. Lacking long professional experience, it is still best to have some credentials as a working journalist.

Also while in college, make an absolute point of absorbing the rules of communications law. This means libel, invasion of privacy, obscenity, and student press law. Lawsuits against school publications are rare but certainly something everyone on a publication should be concerned with. High school advisers have to know their own rights, the rights of their students, and the rights of administrators. Deep trouble can await a teacher ignorant of journalism law.

Deep satisfaction, however, can be the other side of the coin. Committed teachers have good lives. Rewards are great in terms of watching students grow and develop. The ultimate thrill for a journalism teacher comes when a former student succeeds as a professional. That is hard to top.

CHAPTER 11

FINDING THAT FIRST JOB

Finding a job is work in itself. You may find yourself writing dozens of letters and making lots of phone calls before getting even one interview. If jobs aren't available, people often don't take the time to interview candidates. But that doesn't mean that you shouldn't try.

In fact, landing an internship requires the same process as finding a career-track position and plenty of effort. You have to sell yourself. Keep in mind that there are a lot of people looking for jobs. You need to give the individual interviewing you the reasons why you would be better than others who might apply.

WRITING A COVER LETTER

The first step is to write a cover letter. Keep it to one page. Write it with great care. Remember, you are looking for a job where writing is the major tool of the trade. If your letter is poorly constructed, filled with spelling or grammatical errors, or uses improper punctuation, you can forget the phone call. It is always amazing to see, out of dozens of applications and resumes, how poorly people introduce themselves in writing. This is your first impression.

In your letter briefly state why you want to work for the employer and what you bring or can offer. Give a brief summary of relevant experience, if any. If not, be honest. State that you are looking for your first job—or internship. If you are willing to take an internship without pay, say that in the letter.

End the letter by stating that you will call in a few days to set an appointment. (Don't get ahead of yourself—give the post office time to deliver your letter before you call. But, at the same time, don't wait too long. You want to call soon after the letter arrives.)

What if you don't know who to write? Pick up the phone and call the media or prospective employer. After all, you are a journalist. Getting information is your career. It is not impressive to receive a job application addressed to a generic person.

YOUR RESUME

Enclose a well-constructed resume of no more than two pages. No, you don't need to have it printed. It should look neat, but employers are not hiring on superficial criteria. What the resume says is what is important.

At the top, type your full name, address, phone number(s), and E-mail address. The first section should state the position desired. For example:

> Position Desired: Unpaid news-related internship with opportunities to demonstrate writing capabilities and to learn more about a career in journalism.

> Position Desired: Beginning job on a newspaper copydesk.

> Position Desired: Beginning job with a public relations firm or agency in Denver, Colorado.

If you have limiting criteria that affect where you can work, be sure to include it in your letter or resume. For example, if you will accept only paid positions as an intern or will work only in Denver because a spouse or family member lives there, say so. There is no reason to spend time interviewing when there is no hope of getting—or taking—a job if it is offered.

Next, summarize any relevant experience. This should be done in a short paragraph. For example:

> Experience: Two summer internships at XYZ Press, working on copydesk, police reporting, selling classified ads.
>
> Sports editor, *The Buffalo,* West High School student newspaper.

Next follows a summary of your work history. As a student, or when seeking a first job, all jobs are important, even the one summer you spent packing groceries. Here is a suggested format:

Work Experience

> May 1999–September 1999: John's Grocery and Meat Market, packing groceries, stocking shelves, cashier.
>
> September 1999–June 2000: Afterschool work at KXYZ Radio, handling phones, photocopying, storing archive audio tapes.

There are those who suggest you list your experience chronologically. Others suggest you start with the most current job, then go backward to show the growth in responsibilities and what you did most recently. The choice is yours.

Then you will follow with "education." List the places you went to school, starting with high school, and degree earned or last year completed, with the years of attendance.

"Extracurricular activities" will be important in early job applications. Later, you will add your community involvements. Include memberships and affiliations, especially those that could be relevant to the job you seek.

Any honors, awards, scholarships? They are important. List those next.

After that, provide a page with the names, addresses, and phone numbers for three to five people who have agreed to give you a reference. It helps to indicate how you know each one. For example: Steven Smith, supervisor at KXYZ Radio. This helps the prospective employer understand how the individual can best answer questions about you.

Once again, be sure you check for spelling, grammar, and punctuation. There are a lot of employers who will simply circle any typo or spelling error and arrange to have a reject letter sent.

ON-LINE JOB OPPORTUNITIES

Although traditional job searches are still effective and add that personal touch, the Internet offers considerable advantages to your career pursuit. Not only can you use on-line job search engines, like Monster.com and Hotjobs.com, to locate positions in journalism, but you can research companies via their websites to see if they are a good fit for your interests and demeanor.

In addition, you can create a template of your resume (PDF is a popular, widely compatible format, though Microsoft Word also is good), and E-mail it as an attachment to prospective employers. Most companies have a *Jobs* section on their website and will offer advice on the best way to forward your resume to them. This does not relieve you of the obligation to write a clear and concise cover letter or to do your research. Make sure your resume is arriving to the right E-mail address.

If high-tech is your field of interest, you can post your resume to any number of Internet services for employers to browse, or post it to your own website. Though this allows you the opportunity to enhance your resume with articles you have written, photos, animation, and detailed graphics, resist the urge to get too flashy. Don't let your message get lost in a storm of sliding marquees and dissolving JPEG images.

RECOMMENDED READING

An almost countless number of books have been written about journalism and related subjects. You can go to the web and check out all of the ones listed here, and find hundreds more on all aspects of this profession and related or support professions. Don't limit your reading to this small list, or even the list that follows. But if you do read just those that are discussed below, you will have a good view of this field.

Dozens of textbooks that survey this profession have been written for high school and college classes. These texts touch on every journalistic topic. One we recommend is virtually the standard in the field. It's *Introduction to Mass Communications* by Agee, et. al. (Addison Wesley Publishing Company, 1996). This is an established and respected title. The authors and their publishers work to keep the book up-to-date, incorporating information about new technologies and other mass media developments. The book is almost encyclopedic, exploring a wide range of topics. If you are interested in a career in journalism or related fields, you will find this book invaluable.

Another recommendation is actually a series of books. Each year the winning entries in the American Society of Newspaper Editors writing and reporting competition are published. This series started in 1979 and has continued through the current year. The *Best Newspaper Writing* series has been edited by Christopher

Scanlan for Bonus Books. Any book in the series will be worth your reading. These are the works of the best American newspaper journalists. Some of the writing is breathtaking. Not only are their winning articles reproduced, but the writers are interviewed on how they researched and wrote their stories. These interviews constitute virtually a college-level course in writing and reporting.

A book similar to those in this series is written by Karen Rothmyer, *Winning Pulitzers: The Story Behind Some of the Best News Coverage of Our Time* (Columbia University Press, 1991). Even though it has an older copyright, this book tells you in their own words how Pulitzer prize winners came up with their stories. The book also chronicles the changes that have occurred in journalism since the prizes were begun.

WRITING ABOUT WRITING

Here is a gem, perhaps the best book ever written about writing. It's *On Writing Well: An Informal Guide to Writing Nonfiction* by William Zinsser (Harper, 1998). It will take you about a half a day to read this book. Take it seriously and it can change your life as a writer. First, it's a perfect example of everything it preaches: simple, uncluttered, clear, witty, concise. It's filled with examples, good and bad, that everyone who writes can relate to.

Most journalists are more familiar with another small book on writing, Strunk & White's *Elements of Style* (Pearson, 2000). This little volume should be on every writer's shelf. But, if you can only have one, make it *On Writing Well*.

Other books you will want to consider include:

Anderson, Rob, and George Killenberg. *Interviewing: Speaking, Listening, and Learning for Professional Life.* Mountain View, CA: Mayfield Publishing, 1998.

Arndt, David. *How to Shoot and Sell Sports Photography.* Amherst, NY: Amherst Media, 1999.

Biagi, Shirley. *Media Impact: An Introduction to Mass Media,* 5th Edition. Belmont, CA: Wadsworth, 2000.

Block, Mervin. *Writing Broadcast News: Shorter, Sharper, Stronger.* Chicago: Bonus Books, 1997.

Blundell, William E. *The Art and Craft of Feature Writing.* New York: Plume, 1988.

Boetig, Donna Elizabeth. *Feminine Wiles: Creative Techniques for Writing Women's Features Stories That Sell.* Clovis, CA: Word Dancer Press, 1998.

Bragg, Rick. *Somebody Told Me: The Newspaper Stories of Rick Bragg.* Tuscaloosa: University of Alabama Press, 2000.

Cutlip, Scott, et. al. *Effective Public Relations.* Englewood Cliffs, NJ: Prentice-Hall, Inc., 1999.

Daly, Charles P. *Magazine Publishing Industry.* Needham Heights, MA: Allyn and Bacon, 1996.

Ferguson, Donald, Jim Patten and Bradley Wilson. *Journalism Today!* Lincolnwood, IL: NTC/Contemporary Publishing Group, Inc., 2000.

Gabler, Neal. *Winchell: Gossip, Power and the Culture of Celebrity.* New York: Vintage Books, 1995.

Garlock, David. *Pulitzer Prize Feature Stories.* Ames: Iowa State University Press, 1998.

Holtz, Shel. *Public Relations on the Net. Winning Strategies to Inform and Influence the Media, the Investment Community, the Government, the Public, and More!* New York: Amacom, 1998.

Kerbel, Matthew R. *If It Bleeds, It Leads: An Anatomy of Television News.* Boulder, CO: Westview Press, 2000.

Kerrane, Kevin, and Ben Yagoda. *The Art of Fact: A Historical Anthology of Literary Journalism.* New York: Touchstone Books, 1998.

Kilian, Crawford. *Writing for the Web.* Bellingham, WA: Self Counsel Press, 2000.

Lerner, Betsy. *The Forest for the Trees: An Editor's Advice to Writers.* New York: Riverhead Books, 2000.

Lindner, Ken. *Broadcasting Realities: Real-Life Issues and Insights for Broadcast Journalists, Aspiring Journalists and Broadcasters.* Chicago: Bonus Books, 1999.

Mankoff, Robert, and David Remnick. *The New Yorker Book of Business Cartoons.* Princeton, NJ: Bloomberg Press, 1998.

Mulligan, Joseph F. *The Mulligan Guide to Sports Journalism Careers.* Lincolnwood, IL: VGM Career Books, 1998.

Mulligan, Joseph F., Kevin T. Mulligan and Kate Mulligan-Strickland. *Sports Journalism Careers.* Lincolnwood, IL: VGM Career Books, 1998.

Murray, Donald Morison. *Writing to Deadline.* Portsmouth, NH: Heinemann Publishing, 2000.

O'Conner, Patricia T. *Words Fail Me: What Everyone Who Writes Should Know About Writing.* San Diego, CA: Harcourt Brace, 1999.

Perry, James M. *A Bohemian Brigade: The Civil War Correspondents Mostly Rough, Sometimes Ready.* New York: John Wiley & Sons, 2000.

Rather, Dan. *Deadlines & Datelines.* New York: William Morrow & Co., 1999.

Rosen, Jay. *What are Journalists For?* New Haven, CT: Yale University Press, 1999.

Ross, Harold Wallace. *Letters from the Editor, The New Yorker's Harold Ross.* New York: Modern Library, 2000.

Royko, Mike. *One More Time: The Best of Mike Royko.* Chicago: University of Chicago Press, 1999.

Satter, James. *Journalists Who Made History.* Minneapolis, MN: Oliver Press, 1998.

Sloan, David and Laird B. Anderson. *Pulitzer Prize Editorials.* Ames: Iowa State University Press, 1994.

Stahl, Lesley. *Reporting Live.* New York: Simon and Schuster, 1999.

Talese, Gay. *The Kingdom and the Power.* New York: Ivy Books, 1993.

Thomas, Helen. *Front Row at the White House: My Life and Times.* New York: Scribner, 1999.

Yudkin, Marcia. *Writing Articles About the World Around You.* Cincinnati, OH: Writers Digest Books, 1998.

SOURCES OF INFORMATION

Here are some other great sources for information you can access on your computer. Today, the Internet offers dozens of sites just keystrokes away, all of which have some exciting material or information on various aspects of journalism careers. Rather than listing a whole lot of websites, we have provided the names of some groups you can enter into your search engine, or you can write to them for career information. While you are at their site, check on scholarships, their foundation programs, and information you want to know as you explore career opportunities in journalism.

American Advertising Federation
1101 Vermont Avenue NW, #500
Washington, DC 20005

American Association of Advertising Agencies
405 Lexington Avenue, 18th Floor
New York, NY 10174

American Society of Newspaper Editors
11690B Sunrise Valley Drive
Reston, VA 20191

This site has a lot of good links to on-line media publications such as *American Journalism Review, Brill's Content, Columbia*

Journalism Review, Editor & Publisher, and links to many other associations in journalism.

Association for Women in Communications
1244 Ritchie Highway, Suite 6
Arnold, MD 21012

Council of Public Relations Firms
11 Pennsylvania Plaza, 5th Floor
New York, NY 10001

This new association has good career resources for you.

Dow Jones Newspaper Fund
P.O. Box 300
Princeton, NJ 08543

This site offers some good career information, including "Journalism Road to Success" and an excellent career guide for minorities.

National Association of Broadcasters
1771 M Street NW
Washington, DC 20036

If you go to this website, be sure to explore the Career Center.

National Cable Television Association
1724 Massachusetts Avenue
Washington, DC 20036

This site offers some excellent hot links to "cool sites."

National Newspaper Association
1010 Glebe Road, Suite 450
Arlington, VA 22201

This site offers a rich list of other sites to contact for career information in a wide range of areas—from writers and editors, to printing press operators, photographers, and others.

National Press Photographers Association, Inc.
3200 Crousdale Drive, #306
Durham, NC 27705

Public Relations Society of America
33 Irving Street
New York, NY 10013

Radio Television News Directors Association
1000 Connecticut Avenue NW, Suite 615
Washington, DC 20036

(See the end of Chapter 2, "The History of Canadian Journalism," for information about Canadian resources.)

APPENDIX C

COLLEGES AND UNIVERSITIES OFFERING JOURNALISM PROGRAMS

The following colleges and universities offer accredited journalism and mass communications programs that have been rigorously examined by their own faculties, through self-assessment, and by their peers, to assess the quality of their academic programs and standards against the quality of comparable institutions. Accreditation is an integral part of most areas of higher education. It is designed to assure students that the quality of their education has been held accountable to high standards. For journalism, accreditation is provided by the Accrediting Council on Education in Journalism and Mass Communications.

There are many fine programs offered by junior colleges and other institutions. It is important that you carefully examine these programs and courses, and that you talk with the faculty members or admission officers of any institution you may be interested in attending to understand how their programs are evaluated against the standards of accreditation. Nearly all of these institutions have websites that will provide you with considerable information, including financial assistance.

ACCREDITED PROGRAMS

Alabama

Auburn University
Journalism Department
Auburn University, AL 36849-5206
B.A. Journalism; B.A. Corporate Journalism

University of Alabama
College of Communication & Information Sciences
Tuscaloosa, AL 35487-0172
Advertising and Public Relations; Journalism;
Telecommunication and Film
B.A. Communication & Information Sciences; M.A.
Communication & Information Sciences

Alaska

University of Alaska, Anchorage
Department of Journalism and Public Communications
3211 Providence Drive
Anchorage, AK 99508
B.A. Journalism

University of Alaska, Fairbanks
Department of Journalism and Broadcasting
P.O. Box 756120, 101 Bunnell
Fairbanks, AK 99775-6120
B.A. Journalism

Arizona

Arizona State University
Walter Cronkite School of Journalism and Telecommunication
Tempe, AZ 85287-1305
B.A. Journalism; B.A. Broadcasting; M.M.C. Mass
Communication

University of Arizona
Department of Journalism
Tucson, AZ 85721
B.A. Journalism

Arkansas

Arkansas State University
College of Communications
P.O. Box 540
State University, AR 72467-0540
B.S. Journalism, Radio-TV

University of Arkansas, Fayetteville
Department of Journalism
Fayetteville, AR 72701-1201
B.A. Journalism; M.A. Journalism

University of Arkansas, Little Rock
Department of Journalism
Little Rock, AR 72204
B.A. Journalism

California

California Polytechnic State University
Department of Journalism
San Luis Obispo, CA 93407
B.S. Journalism

California State University, Chico
Department of Journalism
207 Tehama Hall
Chico, CA 95929-0600
B.A. Journalism

California State University, Fresno
Department of Mass Communication and Journalism
2225 East San Ramon M/S 10
Fresno, CA 93740-8029
B.A. Mass Communication and Journalism; M.A. Mass
Communication

California State University, Fullerton
Department of Communications
800 North State College Boulevard
Fullerton, CA 92834-6846
B.A. Communications

California State University, Northridge
Department of Journalism
18111 Nordhoff Street
Northridge, CA 91330-8311
B.A. Journalism; M.A. Mass Communication

San Francisco State University
Department of Journalism
1600 Holloway Avenue
San Francisco, CA 94132
B.A. Journalism

San Jose State University
School of Journalism and Mass Communications
San Jose, CA 95192-0055
B.S. Journalism; B.S. Advertising; B.S. Public Relations; M.S.
Mass Communications

University of California
Graduate School of Journalism
121 North Gate Hall #5860
Berkeley, CA 94720-5860
M.J. Journalism

University of Southern California
School of Journalism
3502 Watt Way, ASC 325
Los Angeles, CA 90089-0281
B.A. Broadcast Journalism; B.A. Print Journalism; B.A. Public
    Relations; B.A. Journalism/East Asian Area Studies; M.A.
    Broadcast Journalism; M.A. Print Journalism; M.A. Strategic
    Public Relations; M.A. International Journalism

Colorado

Colorado State University
Department of Journalism and Technical Communication
Fort Collins, CO 80523
B.A. Journalism

University of Colorado
School of Journalism and Mass Communication
Campus Box 478
Boulder, CO 80309
Advertising; Broadcast; News/Editorial
B.S. Journalism; M.A. Journalism

District Of Columbia

American University
School of Communication
Washington, DC 20016-8017
Journalism; Public Communication. B.A. Communication:
    Journalism; B.A. Communication: Public Communication;

M.A. Journalism and Public Affairs; M.A. Public
Communication

Howard University
Department of Journalism
Washington, DC 20059
B.A. Journalism
Department of Radio-TV-Film
B.A. Broadcast Production and Telecommunications
Management

Florida

Florida A&M University
Division of Journalism
Tallahassee, FL 32307
B.S.J. Journalism

Florida International University
School of Journalism and Mass Communication
North Miami, FL 33181
B.S. Communication; M.S. Mass Communication

University of Florida
College of Journalism and Communications
Gainesville, FL 32611-8400
B.S. Journalism; B.S. Advertising; B.S. Telecommunication; B.S.
Public Relations; M.A. Mass Communication

University of Miami
School of Communication
Coral Gables, FL 33124-2030
Advertising Communication and Public Relations; Broadcasting
and Broadcast Journalism; Journalism and Photography
B.S. Communication; M.A. Journalism

University of South Florida
School of Mass Communications
4202 East Fowler Ñ CIS 1040
Tampa, FL 33620
B.A. Mass Communications; M.A. Mass Communications

Georgia

University of Georgia
Henry W. Grady College of Journalism and Mass
    Communication
Athens, GA 30602-3018
A.B.J. Journalism; M.A. Journalism; M.A. Mass Communication

Hawaii

University of Hawaii at Manoa
Department of Journalism
Honolulu, HI 96822-2217
B.A

Illinois

Eastern Illinois University
Department of Journalism
600 Lincoln Avenue
Charleston, IL 61920-3099
B.A. Journalism

Northwestern University
Medill School of Journalism
Fisk Hall, 1845 Sheridan Road
Evanston, IL 60208
B.S.J. Journalism; M.S. Integrated Marketing Communications;
    M.S.J. Journalism

Southern Illinois University
Carbondale School of Journalism
Carbondale, IL 62901-6601
B.S. Journalism

University of Illinois at Urbana-Champaign
College of Communications
810 South Wright Street
Urbana, IL 61801
B.S. Advertising; B.S. Media Studies; B.S. Journalism including
Broadcast Journalism; M.S. Advertising; M.S. Journalism
including Broadcast Journalism

Indiana

Ball State University
Department of Journalism
Muncie, IN 47306
B.A. Journalism; B.S. Journalism; B.A. Advertising; B.S.
Advertising; B.A. Public Relations; B.S. Public Relations

Indiana University
School of Journalism
Bloomington, IN 47405
B.A. Journalism; M.A. Professional

Iowa

Drake University
School of Journalism and Mass Communication
Des Moines, IA 50311
B.A. Journalism and Mass Communication

Iowa State University of Science and Technology
Greenlee School of Journalism and Communication
Ames, IA 50011
B.A. Journalism and Mass Communication including Electronic
Media Studies; B.A. Advertising; B.S. Journalism and Mass
Communication including Science Communication; M.S.
Journalism and Mass Communication

University of Iowa
School of Journalism and Mass Communication
Iowa City, IA 52242
B.A. Journalism; B.S. Journalism; M.A. Professional

Kansas

Kansas State University
A.Q. Miller School of Journalism and Mass Communications
Manhattan, KS 66506
B.A. Mass Communications; B.S. Mass Communications; M.S.
Mass Communications

University of Kansas
William Allen White School of Journalism and Mass
Communications
Lawrence, KS 66045
B.S. Journalism; M.S. Journalism

Kentucky

Murray State University
Department of Journalism and Mass Communications
Box 9
Murray, KY 42071-0009
B.A.; B.S. Journalism, Advertising, Public Relations, and Radio-
TV

University of Kentucky
School of Journalism and Telecommunications
Lexington, KY 40506-0042
B.A. or B.S. Communications (Journalism; Integrated Strategic
  Communication; Telecommunications)

Western Kentucky University
School of Journalism and Broadcasting
Bowling Green, KY 42101-3576
B.A. Advertising; B.A. Photojournalism; B.A. Print Journalism;
  B.A. Public Relations

Louisiana

Grambling State University
Department of Mass Communication
P.O. Box 45
Grambling, LA 71245
B.A. Mass Communication

Louisiana State University
Manship School of Mass Communication
Baton Rouge, LA 70803
B.A. Mass Communication; M. Mass Communication

McNeese State University
Department of Mass Communication
Lake Charles, LA 70609-0335
B.S. Mass Communication

Nicholls State University
Department of Mass Communication
Thibodaux, LA 70310
B.A. Mass Communication

Northwestern State University
Department of Journalism
P.O. Box 5273
Natchitoches, LA 71497
B.A. Journalism

Southern University
Department of Mass Communications
Baton Rouge, LA 70813
B.A. Journalism; M.A. Journalism

University of Louisiana at Lafayette
Department of Communication
P.O. Box 43650
Lafayette, LA 70504-3650
B.A.; M.S.

University of Louisiana at Monroe
Department of Mass Communications
Monroe, LA 71209-0322
B.A. Journalism; B.A. Radio
Television, and Film; B.A. Photojournalism

Maryland

University of Maryland
College of Journalism
College Park, MD 20742
B.A. Journalism; M.A. Journalism

Michigan

Central Michigan University
Department of Journalism
Mount Pleasant, MI 48859
B.A. Journalism; B.S. Journalism

Michigan State University
School of Journalism
East Lansing, MI 48824-1212
B.A. Journalism; M.A. Journalism

Minnesota

St. Cloud State University
Department of Mass Communications
St. Cloud, MN 56301-4498
B.S. Mass Communications; M.S. Mass Communications

University of Minnesota
School of Journalism and Mass Communication
Minneapolis, MN 55455-0418
B.A. Journalism-Professional Program

Mississippi

Jackson State University
Department of Mass Communications
P.O. Box 18590
Jackson, MS 39217
B.S. Mass Communications; M.S. Mass Communications

University of Mississippi
Department of Journalism
University, MS 38677-1848
B.A. Journalism; B.A. Radio/Television

University of Southern Mississippi
Department of Journalism
Box 5121
Hattiesburg, MS 39406-5121
B.A. Journalism; B.A. Advertising

Missouri

University of Missouri-Columbia
School of Journalism
103 Neff Hall
Columbia, MO 65211
B.J. Journalism; M.A. Journalism

Montana

The University of Montana
School of Journalism
Missoula, MT 59812
B.A. Journalism; B.A. Radio-Television; M.A. Journalism

Nebraska

University of Nebraska
College of Journalism and Mass Communications
Lincoln, NE 68588-0127
B.J. Journalism

Nevada

University of Nevada-Reno
Donald W. Reynolds School of Journalism
Reno, NV 89557-0040
B.A. Journalism; M.A. Journalism

New Mexico

New Mexico State University
Department of Journalism and Mass Communications
MSC 3J, P.O. Box 30001
Las Cruces, NM 88003-8001
B.A. Journalism

University of New Mexico
Department of Communication and Journalism
Albuquerque, NM 87131-1171
Journalism and Mass Communication
B.A. Journalism; B.A. Communication

New York

Columbia University
Graduate School of Journalism
New York, NY 10027
M.S. Journalism

New York University
Department of Journalism and Mass Communication
10 Washington Place
New York, NY 10003
B.A. Journalism; M.A. Journalism (Broadcast, Newspaper,
Magazine, Cultural Reporting, and Criticism Sequences);
M.A. Journalism and Latin American-Caribbean Studies; M.A.
Business and Economic Reporting; M.A. Journalism and
French; M.A./M.S. Biomedical Journalism; M.A. Science and
Environmental Reporting; M.A. Journalism and Near Eastern
Studies

Syracuse University
S.I. Newhouse School of Public Communications
Syracuse, NY 13244
B.S. Public Communications; M.A. Public Communications;
M.S. Public Communications

North Carolina
University of North Carolina
School of Journalism and Mass Communication
Chapel Hill, NC 27599-3365
A.B. Journalism and Mass Communication; M.A. Journalism and
   Mass Communication

Ohio

Bowling Green State University
Department of Journalism
Bowling Green, OH 43403
B.S. Journalism

Kent State University
School of Journalism and Mass Communication
Kent, OH 44242-0001
B.A. Journalism and Mass Communication; B.S. Journalism and
   Mass Communication; M.A. Journalism and Mass
   Communication

Ohio State University
School of Journalism and Communication
Columbus, OH 43210-1339
B.A. Journalism; M.A. Journalism

Ohio University
E.W. Scripps School of Journalism
Athens, OH 45701
B.S. Journalism; M.S. Journalism

Oklahoma

Oklahoma State University
School of Journalism and Broadcasting
Stillwater, OK 74078-0195
B.S. and B.A. Journalism

University of Oklahoma
Gaylord College of Journalism and Mass Communication
Norman, OK 73019
B.A.J. Journalism; M.A. Journalism and Mass Communication

Oregon

University of Oregon
School of Journalism and Communication
1275 University of Oregon
Eugene, OR 97403-1275
B.A. Journalism; B.S. Journalism; M.A. Journalism; M.S.
Journalism

Pennsylvania

Pennsylvania State University
College of Communications
201 Carnegie Building
University Park, PA 16802
B.A. Journalism; B.A. Film/Video; B.A. Advertising/Public
Relations; B.A. Telecommunications; B.A. Media Studies;
M.A. Telecommunications Studies

Temple University
Department of Journalism, Public Relations, and Advertising
Philadelphia, PA 19122
B.A. Journalism; M.J. Journalism

South Carolina

University of South Carolina
College of Journalism and Mass Communications
Columbia, SC 29208
B.A. Journalism; M. Mass Communications; M.A.

Winthrop University
Department of Mass Communication
Rock Hill, SC 29733-0001
B.A. Broadcasting; B.A. Journalism

South Dakota

South Dakota State University
Department of Journalism and Mass Communication
Brookings, SD 57007
B.A. Journalism; B.S. Journalism

University of South Dakota
Department of Mass Communication
Vermillion, SD 57069-2390
B.A. Mass Communication; B.S. Mass Communication

Tennessee

East Tennessee State University
Department of Communication
Johnson City, TN 37614-0667
B.A. Mass Communications; B.S. Mass Communications

Middle Tennessee State University
College of Mass Communication
Murfreesboro, TN 37132
B.S. Mass Communication; M.S. Mass Communication

University of Memphis
Department of Journalism
Memphis, TN 38152
B.A. Journalism; M.A. Journalism

University of Tennessee
College of Communications
Knoxville, TN 37996-0332
B.S. Communications; M.S. Communications

University of Tennessee at Chattanooga
Department of Communication
Chattanooga, TN 37403-2598
B.A.

University of Tennessee at Martin
Department of Communications
Martin, TN 38238-5099
B.A.; B.S.

Texas

Baylor University
Department of Journalism
P.O. Box 97353
Waco, TX 76798-7353
B.A. Journalism

Texas A&M University
Department of Journalism
College Station, TX 77843-4111
B.A. Journalism; B.S. Journalism; B.S. Agricultural Journalism

Texas Christian University
Department of Journalism
TCU Box 298060
Ft. Worth, TX 76129
B.A. News-Editorial Journalism, International Communication;
B.S. News-Editorial Journalism, Advertising-Public Relations,
Broadcast Journalism; M.S. Journalism

Texas Tech University
School of Mass Communications
Lubbock, TX 79409-3082
B.A. Journalism; B.A. Advertising; B.A. Public Relations; B.A.
Telecommunications; B.A. Photo Communications

Texas Woman's University
Program in Mass Communications
P.O. Box 425828
Denton, TX 76204-5828
B.A. Mass Communications; B.S. Mass Communications

University of North Texas
Department of Journalism and Mayborn Graduate Institute of
Journalism
P.O. Box 311460
Denton, TX 76203-1460
B.A. Journalism; B.S. Journalism; M.A. Journalism; M.J.
Journalism

University of Texas
Department of Journalism
Austin, TX 78712
B.J. Journalism

Utah

Brigham Young University
Department of Communications
Room E509
Harris Fine Arts Center
Provo, UT 84602-6404
Marketing Communications; Print and Broadcast Journalism;
Public Relations; Communication Studies. B.A.
Communications

University of Utah
Department of Communication
255 South Central Campus Drive
Room 2400
Salt Lake City, UT 84112
B.A. Mass Communication; B.S. Mass Communication; M.A.
Mass Communication; M.S. Mass Communication

Virginia

Hampton University
Department of Mass Media Arts
Hampton, VA 23668
B.A. Mass Media Arts

Norfolk State University
Department of Mass Communications and Journalism
Norfolk, VA 23504
B.A. Mass Communications; B.S. Journalism

Washington and Lee University
Department of Journalism and Mass Communications
Lexington, VA 24450
B.A.

Washington

University of Washington
School of Communications
Box 353740
Seattle, WA 98195-3740
Journalism
B.A. Arts and Sciences

West Virginia

Marshall University
W. Page Pitt School of Journalism and Mass Communications
Huntington, WV 25755
B.A. Journalism; M.A. Journalism

West Virginia University
Perley Isaac Reed School of Journalism
Morgantown, WV 26506-6010
B.S. Journalism; M.S. Journalism

Wisconsin

Marquette University
College of Communication
Milwaukee, WI 53201-1881
B.A. Advertising, Broadcast and Electronic Communication,
Journalism, Public Relations; M.A. Advertising, Broadcast and
Electronic Communication, Journalism, Public Relations

University of Wisconsin-Eau Claire
Department of Communication and Journalism
Eau Claire, WI 54702-4004
Advertising; Broadcast Journalism; Electronic Media; Print
Journalism; Public Relations. B.A.; B.S.

University of Wisconsin-Oshkosh
Department of Journalism
Oshkosh, WI 54901-8696
B.A. Journalism; B.S. Journalism

University of Wisconsin-River Falls
Department of Journalism
River Falls, WI 54022
B.A. Journalism; B.S. Journalism

International

Pontificia Universidad Católica de Chile
School of Journalism
Avenida Jaime Guzmán Errázuriz
3.300-Providencia
Santiago, Chile
Licentiate in journalism; professional title in journalism

SCHOLASTIC MEDIA ASSOCIATIONS, ADVISER GROUPS

This section lists associations and their addresses for students and their advisers that are national in scope and in nearly every state. Many associations have included their websites. While most listings include information on scholarships and workshops, this information is not complete. If you are interested in a specific association, write to it. Many also will have career information available. We appreciate the Journalism Education Association's (JEA) permission to edit this list from their website. JEA was founded in 1924, has more than two thousand members, and is headquartered at Kansas State University. Their mission is to support free and responsible scholastic journalism. The JEA also maintains a bookstore on-line that offers many books of interest.

NATIONAL ASSOCIATIONS

Association for Education in Journalism and Mass Communication (AEJMC)
621 College Street
University of South Carolina
Columbia, SC 29208-0251
aejmc@sc.edu
http://www.aejmc.sc.edu/online/home.html

Columbia Scholastic Press Association (CSPA)
Columbia University
U.S. Mail Only: CMR 5711
2960 Broadway
New York, NY 10027-6902
FEDEX, UPS Only: 90 Morningside Drive
New York, NY 10027
cspa@columbia.edu
http://www.columbia.edu/cu/cspa

Members: Student newspapers, magazines, video and yearbooks
in schools and colleges
Publication: *Student Press Review* (quarterly)

Columbia Scholastic Press Advisers Association (CSPAA)
National Headquarters: CSPA (see above)
cspa@columbia.edu
http://www.columbia.edu/cu/cspa

Members: Advisers, journalism teachers, and former advisers in
noncommercial work for student press
Workshops, Conferences: Annual meeting in March, Columbia
University, New York; semiannual executive board meetings in
March and November at CSPA conventions, Columbia Univer-
sity, New York
Scholarship, Award: James F. Paschal Award, annual (March),
for state press association directors

Dow Jones Newspaper Fund Inc. (DJNF)
P.O. Box 300
Princeton, NJ 08543-0300
609-452-2820/Fax 609-520-5804
newsfund@wsj.dowjones.com
http://www.dowjones.com/newsfund

Publications: *Adviser Update; The Journalist's Road to Success:
A Career and Scholarship Guide; Newspapers, Diversity and You*

Future Journalists of America
P.O. Box 488
Norman, OK 73070

Journalism Education Association (JEA)
Kansas State University
103 Kedzie Hall
Manhattan, KS 66506-1505
jea@ksu.edu (headquarters)
http://www.jea.org/
JEA Press Rights Page: *http://laika.ed.csuohio.edu/students/*
  bowen/jea.html

Members: Journalism teachers, publication advisers, libraries, departments of journalism, media professionals, college students. Fees: Teacher/adviser, associate, $45/year; affiliate, institution: $50/year; retired teacher/adviser, $30/year; college student, $35/year; lifetime, $450

Publications: *Communication: Journalism Education Today (C:JET),* quarterly; *NewsWire* newsletter, quarterly; *JEA Membership Directory; Certification Directory; JEA Bookstore Catalog* (discounts to members); subscription to *Student Press Law Center Report* included in membership fee

Scholarships: National High School Journalist of the Year (Sister Rita Jeanne Scholarships), state winners' portfolio due at JEA, March 15 deadline, $2,000 first place, $1,000 second and third places; Multicultural Outreach Program for advisers; convention registration fee waivers for minority students; scholarships are awarded journalism students at the schools of Yearbook Adviser of the Year and Distinguished Yearbook Adviser winners

Awards: Student Journalist Impact Award, $1,000, March 1 deadline; Carl Towley Award, Medal of Merit, Media Citation, Lifetime Achievement Award, July 1 deadline; National Yearbook Adviser of the Year, mid-October deadline

National Elementary Schools Press Association (NESPA)
Carolina Day School
1345 Hendersonville Road
Asheville, NC 28803
info@nespa.org
http://www.nespa.org

Members: Elementary and middle schools
Publications: Newspaper, how-to book, member directory
Other: Student articles for syndication

National Scholastic Press Association (NSPA)
University of Minnesota
2221 University Avenue SE, Suite 121
Minneapolis, MN 55414
info@studentpress.journ.umn.edu
http://studentpress.journ.umn.edu

Members: Students, student publications
Publication: *Trends in High School Media,* quarterly
Scholarships, Awards: All American, Pacemaker Award, Story
of the Year, Picture of the Year, Multicultural Journalism Award,
All American Photographer, All American Scholar

Quill and Scroll Society (Q & S)
School of Journalism and Mass Communications
The University of Iowa
Iowa City, IA 52242-1528
quill-scroll@uiowa.edu
http://www.uiowa.edu/~quill-sc

Members: Students, teachers
Publications: *Quill & Scroll* magazine, quarterly during school
year; also available are books, charms, pins, awards, and certifi-
cates
Scholarships: Edward J. Nell Memorial Scholarship for students
planning to major in journalism (must be a national winner in
either International Writing/Photography Contest or Yearbook

Excellence Contest in order to apply). Lester G. Benz Memorial Scholarship, for journalism teacher/adviser to upgrade journalism skills—write for deadlines.
Contests: International Writing, Photo Contest; Yearbook Excellence Contest, November 1 deadline

Student Press Law Center (SPLC)
1101 Wilson Boulevard, Suite 1910
Arlington, VA 22209
splc@splc.org
http://www.splc.org

Members: Student journalists, advisers, media professionals
Publications: *Student Press Law Center Report,* three times a year; *Law of the Student Press;* other miscellaneous publications on student media law topics
Scholarships, Awards: Internships for law and journalism students; Scholastic Press Freedom Award
Other: Offers free advice, opinions on any media law topic; evaluation or development of publications guidelines; speaking at journalism seminars and workshops; guidance during litigation

REGIONAL ASSOCIATIONS

Capital Area Youth Journalism Exchange
P.O. Box 3036
Silver Spring, MD 20918-3036

Great Lakes Interscholastic Press Association (GLIPA)
School of Mass Communication
Bowling Green State University
302 West Hall
Bowling Green, OH 43403-0237
http://ernie.bgsu.edu/~lglomsk/GLIPA

Members: Staffs and advisers of schools in Ohio, Indiana, and Michigan
Workshops, Conferences: Yearly two-day retreat for advisers, September/October; annual fall high school journalism workshop, September/October; mass communications week at BGSU, April; spring awards banquet, May; summer workshop
Scholarships: Dorothy Kratz and Forrest Fritz Memorial Scholarships for prejournalism majors who plan to attend BGSU, deadline April 1

New England Scholastic Press Association
Boston University
College of Communication
640 Commonwealth Avenue
Boston, MA 02215

Southern Interscholastic Press Association (SIPA)
College of Journalism and Mass Communications
University of South Carolina
Columbia, SC 29208

Members: Publications (advisers and students)
Publication: *Accents*, newsletter during school year
Scholarships: Locklear Scholarship, Savedge Memorial Scholarship, Savedge Fellowships, January 31 deadline; SIPA Scholarship
Awards: State Press Association awards for best SIPA newspapers, Scroggins Awards, January 31 deadline for the following: Principal of the Year, Freedom of the Press Award, Distinguished Service Awards

Yankee Press Education Network (Yankee PEN)
University of Massachusetts Boston
McCormack 3/613, 100 Morrissey Boulevard
Boston, MA 02125

Publication: *Yankee Scribe,* quarterly
Workshops, Conferences: An annual convention held in a major New England city, plus summer workshops and other special programs.
Scholarship: The John C. "Chips" Quinn Jr. Memorial Scholarship is presented annually to a minority student journalist, deadline early spring

Young DC

2025 Pennsylvania Avenue NW, Suite 321
Washington, DC 20006

Publication: *Young DC,* monthly newspaper written by and for teens in the metropolitan Washington, DC, area
Other: The former Youth News Service/Youth Communication is transitioning into a home page/Internet service and no longer exists as a national student wire news service.

STATE ASSOCIATIONS

Alabama

Alabama Scholastic Press Association (ASPA)

P.O. Box 2389
Tuscaloosa, AL 35403
Delivery Address: 923 University Boulevard
Tuscaloosa, AL 35487
aspa@sa.ua.edu

Members: Teachers, students, media professionals
Publication: *ASPA News,* five times a year
Workshops, Conferences: Fall regional workshops, September; ASPA state convention, March; "The Long Weekend" summer workshop

Scholarships, Awards: Journalist of the Year, Adviser of the Year, Administrator of the Year, deadline February 1

Alaska

Alaska High School Journalism Teachers
Department of Journalism and Broadcasting
University of Alaska
P.O. Box 756120
Fairbanks, AK 99775-6120
http://137.229.14.99/jbwww.html

Summer Workshop: Media Literacy Workshop
Scholarships: Numerous scholarships available, February deadline

Alaska JEA (AJEA)
P.O. Box 672395
Chugiak, AK 99567
Members: Advisers

Arizona

Arizona Interscholastic Press Association
Chandler High School
350 North Arizona Avenue
Chandler, AZ 85224

Arkansas

Arkansas High School Press Association (AHSPA)
Arkansas Scholastic Press Association
1701 Broadway
Little Rock, AR 72206-1249
TheASPA@aol.com

Members: $10 per publication; $5 per adviser
Publication: *ahspa@comp.uark.edu,* monthly

Contests: Many mail-in and on-site publication and individual categories
Summer Workshop: Arkansas Publications Workshop, Fayetteville, for students and advisers; newspaper, yearbook, and photography sequences; scholarships available

Arkansas Journalism Advisers Association (AJAA)

University of Arkansas
747 West Dickson, Suite 5
Fayetteville, AR 72701
ahspa@comp.uark.edu

California

California Scholastic Press Association (CSPA)

2005 Faymont Avenue
Manhattan Beach, CA 90266

Members: Primarily media professionals; some teachers
Workshop, Conference: CSPA-Cal Poly San Luis Obispo Journalism Workshop, open to students nationwide
Scholarship: CSPA scholarship, $700, high school seniors in Southern California are eligible

Journalism Education Association of Northern California (JEANC)

3055 West Princeton
Stockton, CA 95204-1340
http://www.dcn.davis.ca.us/~jeanc/home.html

Members: Journalism teachers (working and retired or former journalism teachers); regular and associate memberships, $30/year or $45/two years
Publication: *JEANC Journal,* quarterly
Summer Workshop: Journalism Academy for students and advisers at University of Pacific, Stockton

Scholarships: High School Journalist of the Year, February 15 deadline; Legislative Scholarship, presented every two years; Multicultural Scholarship, available during convention to pay registration fee

San Joaquin Valley Scholastic Press Association
California State University at Fresno
Department of Mass Communications and Journalism
225 East San Ramon
Fresno, CA 93740-0010

Southern California JEA
Camarillo High School
4660 Mission Oaks Boulevard
Camarillo, CA 93012

Members: $10 per school
Publication: *Communicator,* three times a year
Contests: Seven regions conduct write-off contests in February or March; Regional winners of news, feature, editorial and sports writing attend state write-off contest; Southern California region conducts contests in seven categories
Scholarships: For high school seniors, April 1 deadline

Colorado

Colorado High School Press Association (CHSPA)
School of Journalism and Mass Communications
University of Colorado
Campus Box 287
Boulder, CO 80309

Members: Advisers, newspapers, and yearbooks, $35/year; patron, $25/year
Publication: *Newsline* newsletter, five times per school year
Conferences: Write for information

Scholarships: Dorothy Greer Scholarship, $1,000, senior on publication staff, February 1 deadline; Diversity Scholarship, $1,000, minority senior on publication staff, February 5 deadline

Florida

Florida Scholastic Press Association Inc. (FSPA)
College of Journalism and Communications
P.O. Box 118400
University of Florida
Gainesville, FL 32611-8400

Members: Publications, business affiliates
Publications: *FSPA Today* newsletter, five times a year; convention information booklet, annually
Workshops, Conferences: Write for information.
Scholarships, Awards: Florida Student Journalist of the Year, seniors, February 9 deadline; Florida Journalism Teacher of the Year, nominated by advisers in each district; Webb-Stapler Scholarship, March 1 deadline

Georgia

Georgia Association of Journalism Directors (GAJD)
College of Journalism and Mass Communication
University of Georgia
Athens, GA 30602-3018

Georgia Scholastic Press Association (GSPA)
College of Journalism and Mass Communication
University of Georgia
Athens, GA 30602-3018
gspa@uga.cc.uga.edu

Members: Schools that enroll their student publications (students are members through schools)
Publication: *The GSPA Bulletin* newsletter, six times a year

Workshop: Fall workshop, November
Scholarships: John E. Drewry GSPA Scholarship (to Georgia Champion High School Journalist if he/she attends UGA Journalism College; if not, to the highest runner-up who does)
Contests: Awards to publications and individual students entered in contests for member schools

Southern Regional Press Institute
Savannah State College
P.O. Box 20634
Savannah, GA 31404

Hawaii

Hawaii Schools Publication Association (HSPA)
Moanalua High School
2825 Ala Jlima Street
Honolulu, HI 96818

Members: Teachers, students, and media professionals
Publications: Newsletter, four times per year
Workshops, Conferences: Fall workshop and annual yearbook banquet

Idaho

Idaho Journalism Advisers' Association (IJAA)
3602 Cobblestone Lane
Idaho Falls, ID 83404

Members: Students and advisers in scholastic journalism programs, i.e., newspaper, yearbook, literary magazine, media production, photography
Workshops, Conferences: Write for dates
Scholarships, Awards: Conference write-off awards and Best-of-Show cash awards; Idaho Journalist-of-the-Year college scholarships

Illinois

Eastern Illinois High School Press Association (EIHSPA)
Journalism Department
Eastern Illinois University
Charleston, IL 61920

Illinois JEA (IJEA)
Journalism Department
Eastern Illinois University
Charleston, IL 61920

Illinois State High School Press Association (ISHSPA)
University of Illinois
Journalism Department
119 Gregory Hall, 810 South Wright
Urbana, IL 61801
Conference: Fall conference

Northern Illinois School Press Association (NISPA)
492 Chesterfield Lane
Vernon Hills, IL 60061

Members: Teachers, advisers
Publications: Newsletters, three times per year
Workshop, Conference: Spring conference
Scholarships: NISPA scholarships, March 15 deadline, students
from member schools eligible
Awards: Individual and publication awards

Scholastic Press Association of Chicago (SPAC)
Roosevelt University
430 South Michigan Avenue
Chicago, IL 60605

Members: Teachers, students, and media professionals; regular
membership, $35; associate, $20

Publication: *SPAC Newsletter,* quarterly
Conferences: Annual Spring Conference, Urban Journalism
Workshop, Roosevelt University
Award: Journalism Teacher of the Year
Scholarships: Two, $500 and $2,000, write for timeline and eligibility

Southern Illinois School Press Association (SISPA)
Coulterville High School
Box 386
Coulterville, IL 62237

Indiana

High School Journalism Institute (HSJI)
School of Journalism
Ernie Pyle Hall 200
Indiana University
Bloomington, IN 47405-6201
http://www.journalism.indiana.edu/HSJI/webpage.html

Members: Teachers, high school students
Publication: *Insight,* three times a year
Workshops: Write for information
Scholarships: Scholarships for in-state minority students to
attend HSJI; scholarship for entering freshman to attend IU; write
for deadline

Indiana High School Press Association (IHSPA)
Franklin College
Pulliam School of Journalism
Shirk Hall, 501 East Monroe Street
Franklin, IN 46131
http://www.franklincoll.edu/jouweb/pub/ihspa.html

Members: Teachers, former teachers, colleges, and yearbook representatives; fees one publication, $15; all school media, $25; associate members, $15
Publications: *Press Review,* six times a year; annual member directory
Workshops and Conferences: Write for information
Scholarships: Undergraduate degree scholarships, ranging from $500 to $1,000 for high school seniors, undergraduates pursuing journalism degree at Franklin College; Terry Vander Hayden Minority Scholarship for Indiana minority students pursuing journalism; Mary Benedict Scholarship for new advisers; Master Teacher Scholarship for experienced advisers
Award: Student Journalist of the Year Award, Indiana winner receives $500 stipend; winning portfolio is entered in the national competition

Iowa

Iowa High School Press Association (IHSPA)
W303 Seashore Hall
School of Journalism
The University of Iowa
Iowa City, IA 52242-1528
IHSPA@uiowa.edu
http://www.uiowa.edu/~ihspa/

Members: Advisers and students
Workshop, Conference: State Conference in October
Scholarships, Awards: Stratton Awards, honor Iowa's top journalism educators and supportive professional media; and Administrator of the Year Awards

Kansas

Journalism Educators of Metropolitan Kansas City (JEMKC)
Lawrence High School
1901 Louisiana
Lawrence, KS 66046

Members: Teachers, students, media associates; **Fee:** $15 before November 1, $25 after November 1
Publication: Newsletter, three times per year
Conferences: Fall workshop, September; Advisers Winter Brunch, February, Spring Awards Night, late April.
Scholarships: $300 JEMKC Excellence in Journalism Scholarships
Special Awards: Opal Heatherly Writing Award, $100 and $50 prizes; William Garrett Photography Award, $100; Sara Ellen Campbell Workshop Scholarships
Contests: Spring contests for newspaper, yearbook, and photography; *Kansas City Star* underwrites and supports newspaper contests

Kansas Scholastic Press Association (KSPA)
200 Stauffer-Flint Hall
School of Journalism
University of Kansas
Lawrence, KS 66045-2350
kspa@kuhub.cc.ukans.edu

Members: Journalism teachers and students
Publication: *Courier* newsletter, five times a year
Workshops, Conferences: High school and junior high school; write for information
Scholarships, Awards: Kansas High School Journalist of the Year; Administrator of the Year

Kentucky

Greater Louisville H.S. Press Association
Bellarmine College
2001 Newburg Road
Louisville, KY 40205-0671

Kentucky High School Press Association
University of Kentucky
218 Grehan Building
Lexington, KY 40506-0042

Louisiana

Louisiana Scholastic Press Association
Manship School of Mass Communications
Louisiana State University
Baton Rouge, LA 70803
http://www.lspa2000.gen-next.com

Membership Dues: $20 first publication, $25 for two, $30 for three

Maryland

Maryland Scholastic Press Association
College of Journalism
University of Maryland
College Park, MD 20742-7111

Members: Advisers and students
Workshops, Conferences: Fall convention, one day, fifty workshop sessions; summer, one-week intensive workshops

Michigan

Michigan Interscholastic Press Association (MIPA)
305 Communication Arts Building
School of Journalism
Michigan State University
East Lansing, MI 48824-1212
http://journalism.msu.edu/mipa

Members: Teachers, schools
Publication: *Stet,* quarterly during school year
Summer Workshop: Early August

Conferences: Spring and fall conference
Scholarships: $250 for "all-MIPA students"; various scholarships for workshop, based on need
Special Awards: Golden Pen (adviser of the year), Administrator of the Year, Student Journalist Team (top high school student journalism in state), top newspaper student, top yearbook student

Minnesota

Journalism Educators of Minnesota (JEM)
1375 85th Court W
Northfield, MN 55057

Members: Secondary journalism educators/advisers and advisers from schools that join Minnesota High School Press Association
Publications: Contribute to MHSPA newsletter
Scholarships, Awards: Student Journalist of the Year, $300 to state winner; recognize Minnesota advisers with ten to thirty years of experience
Workshops: On-site instruction in editors training, desktop publishing, writing, design

Minnesota High School Press Association (MHSPA)
University of Minnesota
620 Rarig Center
330 21st Avenue S
Minneapolis, MN 55455
http://www.studentpress.journ.umn.edu

Mississippi

Mississippi Scholastic Press Association (MSPA)
Department of Journalism
University of Mississippi
331 Farley Hall
University, MS 38677

Members: High school teachers and students
Publications: Newsletter, annual
Workshops, Conferences: Fall regional workshops in Tupelo and Jackson; statewide conference at University of Mississippi in April

Missouri

Central Missouri Journalism Educators Association
Windsor H.S.
210 North Street
Windsor, MO 64360

Journalism Educators of Metropolitan Kansas City (JEMKC)
Lawrence High School
1901 Louisiana
Lawrence, KS 66046

Members: Teachers, students, media associates; fee $15 before November 1, $25 after
Publication: Newsletter, three times a year
Conferences: Fall workshop in September; Advisers' Winter Brunch in February; Spring Awards Night
Scholarships: Three $300 JEMKC Excellence in Journalism Scholarships
Special Awards: Opal Heatherly Writing Award, $100, $50 prizes; Bill Garrett Photography Award, $100 in prizes; Sarah Ellen Campbell workshop scholarships
Contests: Spring contest for newspaper, yearbook, and photography; *The Kansas City Star* underwrites and supports the newspaper and writing contests

Missouri Interscholastic Press Association (MIPA)
Missouri School of Journalism
76 Gannett Hall
Columbia, MO 65211
jouramr@muccmail.missouri.edu

Members: Teachers
Publications: *MIPA News-Gram,* quarterly
Conference and Summer Workshop: High School Journalism Day, write for information; Summer Media Workshop
Scholarship: Missouri Student Journalist of the Year

Southeast Missouri Student Press Association (SEMSPA)
    Southeast Missouri State University
    Cape Girardeau, MO 63701

    Members: Teachers and students; $10 per publication plus $3 per student annually
    Workshop: Fall workshop at Southeast Missouri University, Cape Girardeau, October
    Scholarship: Scholarship to a student or adviser for summer workshop, May deadline
    Contents: Writing, photography, layout and design, and current events contests

Montana

Montana Interscholastic Press Association
    School of Journalism
    University of Montana
    Missoula, MT 59812

Nebraska

Nebraska High School Press Association
    College of Journalism and Mass Communications
    University of Nebraska at Lincoln
    206 Avery Hall
    Lincoln, NE 68588-0134

New Jersey

Garden State Scholastic Press Association
73 Lincoln Street
Jersey City, NJ 07307

New Mexico

New Mexico Scholastic Press Association (NMSPA)
9905 Chapala NE
Albuquerque, NM 87111

Members: Teachers, advisers, media professionals, university professors
Publication: NMSPA *Adviser,* newsletter, quarterly
Workshops, Conferences: Fall Media Festival, September; State Spring Conference, March
Scholarships, Awards: New Mexico High School Journalist of the Year; New Mexico High School Journalism Hall of Fame; Administrator of the Year; Friend of Journalism and adviser awards

New York

Empire State Scholastic Press Association (ESSPA)
Syracuse University
310 Newhouse One
Syracuse, NY 13244

Members: Teachers, students
Workshops, Conferences: Fall conference, October; Summer School Press Institute, last week in July; Syracuse Press Day, in spring with Syracuse newspapers NIE; a series of spring regional workshops
Scholarships: Two scholarships awarded to Syracuse University from high school members

New York City Scholastic Press Association
Department of Journalism and Mass Communications
New York University
10 Washington Place, Fifth Floor
New York, NY 10003

Western New York School Press Association
Hendrix Hall
State University of New York at Fredonia
Fredonia, NY 14063

North Carolina

North Carolina Scholastic Media Association (NCSMA)
CB#3365, 13D Howell Hall
University of North Carolina-Chapel Hill
School of Journalism and Mass Communications
Chapel Hill, NC 27599-3365
http://sunsite.unc.edu/ncsma

Members: Publications advisers/journalism teachers, students
Publications: The NCSMA *Scoop* newsletter, five times a year
Workshops, Conferences: Scholastic Media Institute, workshops in broadcasting, desktop publishing, magazine, newspaper, photojournalism, and yearbook; other regional workshops—write for information
Scholarship, Award: North Carolina Journalism Student of the Year (with JEA), $100 to state winner

North Dakota

Northern Interscholastic Press Association
School of Communication
University of North Dakota
P.O. Box 7169
Grand Forks, ND 58202

Members: Teachers and students by publication

Publications: Newsletter, monthly
Workshops, Conference: Fall workshops, spring conference
Scholarships: Grand Forks Herald Scholarship, Forum (Fargo-Moorhead) Scholarship, Bismarck Tribune Scholarship
Award: Adrian Dunn Adviser of the Year Award

Ohio

Journalism Association of Ohio Schools (JAOS)
Ohio State University
School of Journalism
242 West 18th Avenue
Columbus, OH 43210

Northeast Ohio Scholastic Press Association (NOSPA)
School of Journalism and Mass Communication
130 Taylor Hall
Kent State University
Kent, OH 44242-0001
http://www.jmc.kent.edu/JMC/smp/

Members: High school publication membership, $40/year covers all contests
Publications: Newsletter, four times per year
Conferences and Summer Workshops: Write for information

Tri-County Journalism Association (TCJA)
6923 Palmyra Road
Warren, OH 44481

Oklahoma

Oklahoma Interscholastic Press Association (OIPA)
P.O. Box 5539
Norman, OK 73070

Members: Teachers and their students, others who are interested—fee (include critique) ranges from $80 early bird to $95 late; retired advisers are free

Publications: *OIPA Reporter* newsletter, three times per year

Conferences: Fall conference, mid-October; spring conference, March

Workshops: Summer workshop for advisers and students in desktop publishing, yearbook, photography, newspaper, early June; adviser and student scholarships available, April deadline; graduate credit available for advisers

Scholarship: McMahon Scholarship for high school senior who must major in journalism at University of Oklahoma, deadline February 15.

Award: Lois A. Thomas Award for Oklahoma journalism teacher of the year

Oregon

Northwest Scholastic Press (NWSP)

Oregon State University
210 Memorial Union East
Corvallis, OR 97331-1618
nwsp@ccmail.orst.edu
http://osu.orst.edu/pubs/nwsp

Members: Oregon teachers/publication advisers

Publications: *imPRESSions* newsletter, quarterly

Workshop, Conference: Fall press day

Scholarships: Oregon High School Journalist of the Year, February 15 deadline, $1,000 for Journalist of the Year, $500 for runner-up

Award: Oregon High School Journalism Teacher of the Year (Mary Hartman Award)

Oregon Journalism Education Association (OJEA)
Silverton High School
802 Schlador Street
Silverton, OR 97381-1099
http://jcomm.uoregon.edu/~ojea
Workshops, Conferences: Write for information
Scholarships, Awards: Oregon Journalism Teacher of the Year;
Oregon High School Journalist of the Year, February deadline

Oregon Scholastic Press Association
School of Journalism and Communications
University of Oregon
Allen Hall 201
Eugene, OR 97403

Pennsylvania

Pennsylvania School Press Association (PSPA)
East High School
450 Ellis Lane
West Chester, PA 19380

Members: School publications staffs
Publications: *Keystoner* newsletter, quarterly; *Legal Pad,* legal
services newsletter
Workshop, Conference: Fall convention and contests
Scholarships, Awards: Student Journalist of the Year, Adminis-
trator of the Year

South Carolina

South Carolina Scholastic Broadcasters Association (SCSBA)
College of Journalism and Mass Communications
University of South Carolina
Columbia, SC 29208
http://www.jour.sc.edu/

Members: Teachers and students
Workshop: Fall workshop
Conference: Spring convention

South Carolina Scholastic Press Association (SCSPA)

College of Journalism and Mass Communications
University of South Carolina
Columbia, SC 29208
http://www.jour.sc.edu/scspa/home.html

Members: Middle school and high school publications staffs
(yearbook, newspaper, magazine)
Publications: *Perspective* newsletter, bi-monthly
Conferences: Spring and fall conference
Scholarships: Two senior scholarships, $500 each, mid-March
deadline
Awards: Journalist of the Year, mid-March deadline; Reid H.
Montgomery Adviser of the Year Award; Albert T. Scroggins
Award

South Dakota

South Dakota High School Press (SDHSP)

SDHSP Journalism and Mass Communications
South Dakota State University
Box 2235
Brookings, SD 57007

Members: Teachers, students
Publication: *High School Editor,* two times a year
Conference: High School Press Day Convention
Workshops: Summer workshops

Tennessee

Tennessee High School Press Association (THSPA)
330 Communications Building
School of Journalism
University of Tennessee
Knoxville, TN 37996-0330
Members: $8
Publications: *Press Ahead* newsletter, quarterly
Conference: THSPA spring conference
Contests: Overall and individual contests in newspaper, yearbook, and magazine categories
Awards: Journalism Teacher of the Year, Distinguished Service Award (teachers)

Texas

Association of Texas Photography Instructors (ATPI)
P.O. Box 121092
Arlington, TX 76012

Members: Photo educators in all curriculum areas (art, journalism, technology education, and vocational education), and other supporters of photo education
Publications: ATPI *Letter* newsletter, quarterly, free subscriptions available
Summer Workshop and Conferences: Write for information
Scholarship: Scholarship to graduating senior based on portfolio of student's work, sponsoring teacher must be ATPI member

Interscholastic League Press Conference (ILPC)
P.O. Box 8028
UT Station
Austin, TX 78713-8028
http://www.utexas.edu/admin/uil/

Members: Schools (teachers and students)
Publications: *Leaguer* newsletter; *ILPC Membership Directory*
Workshops, Conferences: Write for information
Scholarship: One $1,000 scholarship per year to student planning to attend a Texas college or university and major in journalism
Awards: Edith Fox King Award, Max R. Haddick Teacher of the Year Award

Panhandle High School Press Association

Art, Communications, and Theatre Department
West Texas A&M University
Box 747, WT Station
Canyon, TX 79016-0001

Members: Teachers and students
Workshop, Conference: Winter conference, December

Texas Association of Journalism Educators (TAJE)

P.O. Box 150185
Austin, TX 78715-0185

Members: Teachers, advisers, $20/year
Publications: *Upfront,* four to five times a year
Contests: Clip contest categories cover writing and design of newspapers, yearbooks, and literary magazines, deadline in December; contests also at state convention
Scholarships: $1,500 and three $500 scholarships for high school students. Winners are announced in April at state scholastic press conference, scholarships are given to up to six students and up to three new advisers for summer workshops.
Special Awards: Texas High School Journalist of the Year, Administrator of the Year
Conference: TAJE state convention held with Association of Texas Photography Instructors the last weekend in October for students and advisers

Texas High School Press Association (THSPA)
Abilene Christian University
Department of Journalism and Mass Communications
ACU Station, Box 7892
Abilene, TX 79699-7892

Publications: Newsletter, periodically
Workshops, Conferences: Write for information

Utah

Utah Journalism Educators Association (UJEA)
Department of Communication
2613 LNCO
University of Utah
Salt Lake City, UT 84112

Members: High school newspaper advisers
Workshops, Conferences: October, during Utah Education
Association conference

Virginia

Virginia High School League Inc. (VHSL)
1642 State Farm Boulevard
Charlottesville, VA 22911-8809

Members: Membership by school for all school activities
Publications: *League Notes*, monthly; *Leaguer*, annually
Workshop: Fall Publications Workshop
Scholarship, Award: Col. Charles E. Savedge Scholarship,
$500, for graduating senior, March 1 deadline

Washington

Washington Journalism Education Association (WJEA)
Gig Harbor High School
5101 Rosedale Street NW
Gig Harbor, WA 98335

Members: Teachers
Publication: *MORE* newsletter, five times a year
Workshops, Conferences: State conference, March; summer
workshop for advisers and students, August
Scholarships: Adviser, (one inexperienced, one experienced),
deadline February 1; students, one newspaper, one yearbook,
three study grants (grades 9–12), deadline February 1
Awards: Dorothy McPhillips Award, Adviser of the Year,
Administrator of the Year, May 15 deadline

West Virginia

United High School Media (UHSM)
Marshall University
315 Smith Hall, Greer Boulevard
Huntington, WV 25755-2622

Members: High school teachers and students
Publication: Newsletter, twice a year
Workshops: Hands-on Workshop, September; Scholastic Journal-
ism Program, October and November—college credit available
Conference: UHSM Convention
Scholarship: Outstanding High School Journalist
Contests: 150 overall and individual contest categories in news-
paper, yearbook, television, radio—December 31 deadline

West Virginia High School Journalism Teachers Association
West Virginia University
P.I. Reed School of Journalism
P.O. Box 6010
Morganton, WV 26506-6010

Members: Teachers and advisers, no membership fee
Contests: Spring competition for students in ten categories, two divisions

Wisconsin

Kettle Moraine Press Association
Continuing Education Services
University of Wisconsin at Whitewater
Whitewater, WI 53190

Northeast Wisconsin Scholastic Press Association
University of Wisconsin at Oshkosh
Department of Journalism
Oshkosh, WI 54901-8696

Urban Journalism Workshop
Marquette University
P.O. Box 1881
Milwaukee, WI 53201-1881

Members: Students only, scholarships available

Wyoming

Wyoming High School Press Association
Box 128
Rock River, WY 82083
Scholarship: High School Journalist of the Year
Workshop: WHSSPA Fall Workshop
Award: Adviser of the Year